NUMBER 122

Yale French Studies

Out of Sight: Political Censorship of the Visual Arts in Nineteenth-Century France

SPECIAL EDITOR: ROBERT JUSTIN GOLDSTEIN

ROBERT JUSTIN GOLDSTEIN	1	Editor's Preface: Political Censorship of the Visual Arts in Nineteenth-Century France
ROBERT JUSTIN GOLDSTEIN	14	Censorship of Caricature and the Theater in Nineteenth-Century France: An Overview
DAVID O'BRIEN	37	Censorship of Visual Culture in France, 1815–1852
JUDITH WECHSLER	53	Daumier and Censorship, 1866–1872
BERTRAND TILLIER	79	The Impact of Censorship on Painting and Sculpture, 1851–1914
DONALD E. ENGLISH	104	Anxiety and the Official Censorship of the Photographic Image, 1850–1900
KAREN L. CARTER	130	The Specter of Working-Class Crowds: Political Censorship of Posters in the City of Paris, 1881–1893
KENNETH GARNER AND RICHARD ABEL	160	Regulating a Risky Business: Film, Censorship, and Public Safety in Prewar France, 1909–1914

Yale French Studies

Robert Justin Goldstein, *Special editor for this issue*

Alyson Waters, *Managing editor*

Editorial board: Thomas Kavanagh (Chair), R. Howard
 Bloch, Edwin Duval, Alice Kaplan, Christopher L.
 Miller, Maurice Samuels, Christopher Semk, Edwige
 Tamalet-Talbayev, Yue Zhuo

Editorial assistant: Mary Anne Lewis

Editorial office: 82-90 Wall Street, Room 308

Mailing address: P.O. Box 208251, New Haven,
 Connecticut 06520-8251

Sales and subscription office:

Yale University Press, P.O. Box 209040

New Haven, Connecticut 06520-0940

Designed by James J. Johnson and set in Trump
 Medieval Roman by Newgen North America.
 Printed in the United States of America by Sheridan
 Books, Ann Arbor, Michigan.

ISSN 044-0078

ISBN for this issue 978-0-300-18528-7

ROBERT JUSTIN GOLDSTEIN

Editor's Preface: Political Censorship of the Visual Arts in Nineteenth-Century France

The English saying that a "picture is worth a thousand words" has often been applied in a perverse manner by the ruling authorities, who have frequently feared visual imagery even more than the printed word. This was especially true in times and places, such as nineteenth-century France, where a large part, and in some cases, a majority, of the population was illiterate and thus could not understand print but could understand visual imagery, including statues, paintings, caricatures, photographs, the cinema, the theater, and so on. Aside from the fact that images were accessible to the illiterate in ways that print was not, the authorities also especially feared the visual arts because they were simply considered more powerful in their impact than the written word. Thus, a French minister warned in 1829 that "engravings and lithographs act immediately upon the imagination of the people, like a book which is read with the speed of light; if it wounds modesty or public decency the damage is rapid and irremediable."[1] Similarly in 1852 the French police minister termed drawings "one of the most dangerous" of all means "used to shake up and destroy the sentiments of reserve and morality essential" for a well-ordered society, especially because "even the worst page in the worst book requires time to be read and a certain degree of intelligence to understand it" while "everyone" could understand a caricature.[2] Thus, in France, prior censorship of the printed word was not enforced after 1822, but caricature censorship lasted until 1881, theater censorship until 1906, and cinema censorship was introduced shortly thereafter.

1. Archives nationales, Paris (AN), F18 2343. My translation.
2. AN, FA 18 2342.

YFS 122, *Out of Sight: Political Censorship of the Visual Arts in Nineteenth-Century France*, ed. Goldstein, © 2012 by Yale University.

Similar views and fears have been expressed in word and action in other nineteenth-century authoritarian states. For example, in successfully urging Prussian King Friedrich Wilhelm IV to reverse in 1843 his recent abolition of censorship of drawings, his interior minister won his case by arguing that caricatures "prepare for the destructive influence of negative philosophies and democratic spokesmen and authors," especially since the "uneducated classes do not pay much notice to the printed word" but do pay attention to caricatures and "understanding them." He added that to "refute a caricature is impossible; its impression is lasting and sometimes ineradicable."[3] Similarly, the late nineteenth-century German journalist Maximilien Harden, a leading critic of Emperor Wilhelm II's authoritarian regime, declared: "No other sort of publication can have such an effect on public opinion as the illustrated satirical magazine, which appeals to the most brilliant and to the simplest mind, and with its scornful challenge and raucous laughter, attracts attention everywhere."[4]

Modern authoritarian regimes have also feared the impact of the visual arts. For example, during the 1987 South Korean elections, which were widely viewed as presaging a liberalization of politics, vice-minister of culture and information Choi Chang Yoen declared: "The impact of works of art is so great that they can hardly be left with unlimited freedom. We have our social and moral values that must be defended and upheld. We will not allow things brought up that are detrimental to our society or our national security." Clandestine copies of hundreds of secret directives issued by the South Korean information ministry to newspapers in 1986 revealed that the government had banned publishing pictures of the leading opposition figures and that a cartoonist was forced to retire after drawing a character resembling President Chun Doo Hwan in alleged violation of the law banning caricatures insulting the head of state.[5]

The purpose of this volume is to provide as comprehensive as possible a collection of information concerning the use of censorship of visual imagery by the authorities in nineteenth-century France using both primary and secondary sources.

---

3. Mary Lee Townsend, *Forbidden Laugther: Popular Humor and the Limits of Repression in Nineteenth-Century Prussia* (Ann Arbor: University of Michigan Press, 1992), 19; 180–81.

4. Anne Allen, *Satire and Society in Wilhelmine Germany: 'Kladderadatsch' and 'Simiplicissimus,' 189–1914* (Lexington, KY: 1984), 41–42, 89.

5. *New York Times*, October 26, 1986; September 20, 1987; *Ann Arbor News*, June 24, 1986; March 26, 1987.

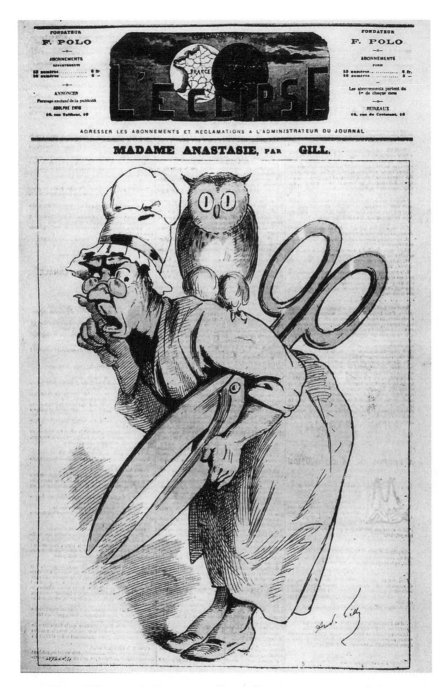

Figure 1. "Madame Anastasie" by André Gill, July 19, 1874, *L'éclipse*. French caricaturists typically depicted censorship as an ugly old hag (although all the censors were male) with a huge pair of scissors. This portrayal is perhaps the most famous ever produced. (Private collection)

In the first essay, I provide a brief summary of our current knowledge about censorship of caricature and of the theater in nineteenth-century France. These two topics are treated together because they were often lumped together by the authorities, and changes in their regulations often were handed down at about the same time, or even in the same legislation. This was especially apparent in 1835 when censorship of both drawings and drama, which had been abolished with the success of the 1830 Revolution, was reinstated at the same time and in the same legislation (the notorious September laws), based on the same argument by Minister of Justice Jean-Charles Persil. His argument, which is quoted at length in this essay, essentially amounted to stating that the visual arts were entirely different from the press, because opinions expressed in the press amounted to a form of thought appealing to the mind, while the visual arts were a form of "*deed*, an *action*, a *behavior*" that spoke directly to the senses, and were especially dangerous when addressed to people "gathered together."[6] This same essay seeks to give a brief history of caricature and drama censorship in nineteenth-century France and to further underline the reasons why they were so feared: they were considered as especially powerful means of communication; they were accessible to the illiterate; and they were often viewed collectively by crowds whom it was feared might take immediate action. Data is presented on when censorship was implemented and terminated and how many plays and drawings were affected. Stress is laid on how valuable censorship is for conveying quite precisely what the government feared and when. Thus, as legislative deputy Robert Mitchell notes, drawings that "displease the government are always forbidden," and in studying this subject "we know exactly what the government fears and what it encourages, we have a clear revelation of its intimate thoughts."[7] Similarly, modern French historian Odile Krakovitch describes theater censorship as providing a "marvelous witness to the preoccupations, mentalities, reflexes, fears, consciences and knowledge of people of the century." One constant ran through the theater and caricature censorship: always, they aimed at preservation of the existing political power structure.[8]

---

6. Archives parlementaires de 1787 à 1860 (Paris, 1908) (emphasis in original).

7. *Journal Officiel*, June 8, 1880, 6234.

8. Odile Krakovitch, "Les ciseaux d'Anastasie: Le théâtre an XIXe siècle," in *Censures: de la Bible aux larmes d'Éros* (Paris: Éditions du centre Pompidon, 1987), 56; 63.

Figure 2. "An Imitator of Don Quixote," by Gilbert-Martin, June 19, 1875, *Le Don Quichotte*. Here, the censor is a Don Quixote in reverse, not tilting at windmills in the search of love and beauty, but seeking to destroy them instead. An accompanying text advised the censor to "destroy an abuse" by plunging her scissors "into your stomach." (Private collection)

Figure 3. The hatred of caricaturists for censorship was boundless. Here in "The Ball," caricaturist Alfred Le Petit likens trying to be a caricaturist under censorship to working with a ball and chain (surmounted by Anastasie) attached to his leg. *Le Grelot*, July 20, 1873. (Private collection)

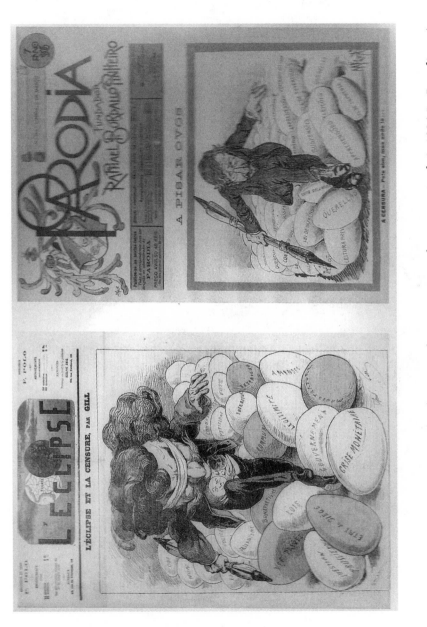

Figure 4. Hatred of caricaturists for the censorship was universal. Here, a March 2, 1906 *La Parodia* caricature published by Raphael Bordallo Pinheiro, has obviously been inspired by an earlier caricature (left) by André Gill in the November 26, 1871 *L'éclipse*. In both, the censured caricaturist is forced to walk on eggs to avoid controversial subjects (in addition, Gill is blindfolded). (National Library of Portugal; private collection)

Figure 5. Although prior censorship of caricature was abolished in 1881, it persisted for the theater until 1906. On December 14, 1901 the journal *Le Rire* published a special issue solely devoted to attacking theater censorship, with Anastasie cutting the wings off an innocent cherub. (Private collection)

David O'Brien, an American art historian, provides, in his essay "Censorship of Visual Culture in France, 1815–1852," a survey of the official censorship of visual culture during the period aside from caricatures and the theater. He argues that recent studies have established that censorship of visual culture occurred during this period throughout France and was remarkably consistent across changes of regimes and forms of government even while varying enormously in relationship to different types of visual culture, revealing much about the government's preoccupations and goals. In addition to well-known cases involving prints, paintings, and sculpture, a whole host of other objects and images was suppressed, from flags, cockades, and hats, to clocks, suspenders, and tobacco boxes decorated with political images, and from jewelry and busts to kerchiefs and pipes. O'Brien notes that the reproducibility of a medium, its cultural prestige, the class affiliation of a perceived audience, and the publicity involved all affected its treatment by the government. The visual production of previous regimes, particularly public sculptures, was also censored, sometimes through officially sanctioned vandalism, although by the time of the July Monarchy the notion of cultural heritage preserved many monuments from destruction. Complementing the argument made in the first essay, O'Brien concludes that while the government was relatively unconcerned with artistic and elite forms of culture, it paid keen and increasing attention to objects belonging to a nascent mass culture that expressed oppositional political messages.

In contrast to the first two essays in this volume, which cover long time periods and a variety of media, in the third essay, American art historian Judith Wechsler provides a case study of one artist and one medium during a short period of time in "Daumier and Censorship, 1866–1872." The essay reviews the censorship laws and changes in their implementation, while focusing on some of Daumier's caricatures, highlighting particularly indicative, characteristic, or significant works, emphasizing those images that make specific reference to the press or censorship. The changes in attitude toward censorship by the government from year to year are juxtaposed with the subjects addressed by Daumier. Wechsler argues that the implementation of censorship during the time period studied became more variant and lenient and that Daumier was therefore able to introduce hitherto forbidden political references into his caricatures. While the government did not articulate the changing censorship criteria during these years, the censors were given greater flexibility in deciding whether to condemn images, reflecting, among other things, frequent changes in top level bureaucratic personnel who handled censorship matters. While their exact criteria remain unknown, Wechsler points out that we can in part deduce them from Daumier's caricatures. But we must also consider how the preclusions of censorship might have made possible certain kinds of artistic achievement, including Daumier's introduction of new figures or forms in order to avoid censorship. In particular, Daumier developed the use of allegory in caricature as a means of subversion, by using suggestion and imagination in both subject and style, turning indirection into direction, and so challenging censorship's constraints.

In "The Impact of Censorship on Painting and Sculpture 1851–1914," French art historian Bertrand Tillier complements O'Brien's work on the first half of the nineteenth century with a sweeping analysis of a wide variety of censored visual art forms not covered in other essays here, such as cinema, caricature, and photography. Tillier argues that although in theory prior press censorship did not exist in France after 1830, in practice "by means of degrees, laws, orders or statutes," as well as sometimes by what amounted to officially-sponsored vandalism, a "harsh political censorship was regularly applied to artists and specific works . . . irrespective of the regime in power." In his contribution, Tillier seeks to discuss the means whereby censorship was employed, "its motivations and applications, the places it was practiced and the resistance and strategies that it sometimes catalyzed among artists."

Like O'Brien, Tillier points out that censorship of images extended far beyond paintings and sculpture to include "drawings, engravings, lithographs, medallions, prints or emblems of any kind," and specifically notes that images of the Commune of all kinds were sweepingly forbidden throughout France, as were songs, pamphlets, and images of all manner. Moreover, artistic images were also forbidden under laws passed between 1889 and 1894 that specifically targeted insults to public decency, heads of state and diplomats, as well as anarchist propaganda. Among the victims of such regulations were hawkers' medallions, cufflinks, pipes, and tobacco jars. Representations of the French Second Republic such as the liberal cock and fasces were replaced by the imperial eagle and busts of Emperor Napoleon III, while after the downfall of the Second Empire a vast variety of Napoleonic images were outlawed, as was the revolutionary depiction of "Marianne" wearing a Phrygian gap. Later, during the

Boulanger crisis, all Boulangist imagery was forbidden. On several occasions works submitted to Salons that were viewed as jeopardizing French foreign relations or as otherwise offensive (for example, if they evoked the Commune or the Dreyfus Affair) were banned, removed, retitled, and so on. As with other forms of visual imagery, invariably the key motive for the censorship acts described by Tillier was that governments of all political hues feared that images were liable to inflame passions; he quotes one journalist as stating that depictions of the "agents of riot and crime as martyrs" was a "reprehensible act" and all such should be "swept away, eliminated, for the sake of morality and public order."

In his contribution, independent scholar Donald English provides an overview of "Anxiety and the Official Censorship of the Photographic Image in Nineteenth-Century France, 1850–1900." English points out that with its 1839 invention by Frenchman Louis Daguerre, photography became one of the most popular inventions in nineteenth-century France, and that during the next decades millions of photographs circulated in a wide variety of formats. These images were easily integrated into French visual culture and soon attracted the attention of political censors, who feared their power to influence and shape attitudes and possibly incite action among French viewers, especially since they were regarded as unmediated copies of "truth" and "reality." English's article examines the efforts of various French officials to limit the flow of photographic images. Among the issues he discusses are the legal justification for censorship, how various press laws applied to the new technology, and assumptions about the propagandistic power and danger of the image. He examines the visual content of censored images and how their circulation was controlled. As French political culture evolved from the Second Empire to the Third Republic, press censorship gradually subsided after 1881, but fear of the photograph did not wane. Illegal censorship resumed whenever the government considered that a photograph posed a serious threat to the social and political order, especially during such crises as the Boulanger and Dreyfus affairs. However, by the turn of the century, with the vast rise in the number of professional press photographers and increased reproduction of photographs in the press, overt censorship became more difficult. Police officials consequently shifted from prior censorship to the control of photographers' access to controversial public and private events whose images might generate adverse public reaction. Overall, anxiety and censorship of the photograph remained constant, while evolving to meet the challenge of advancing technology and the modernization of the popular press.

In her piece, American art historian Karen Carter discusses the rarely-studied subject of "The Specter of Working-Class Crowds: The Censorship of Political Posters in Late Nineteenth-Century Paris." Carter points out that historians of this period have often characterized the changes brought about by modernity (both in relation to public life and urban spaces) as resulting in the withering of public engagement with politics and the atomization of the individual. This sense of disengagement from public life was particularly acute in the decades following France's humiliating defeat in the Franco-Prussian War, the harsh suppression of the French Commune and the intense commercialization of Paris following Haussmannization. The reasons for the depolitcization of late nineteenth-century "public culture" include the withdrawal of the bourgeoisie from the public sphere, the rise of commercial mass media, and the encroachment of capital into every facet and space of daily life. Rather than considering the overarching economic issues related to the development of capitalism, Carter's essay discusses another, less frequently examined cause for the depolitcization of culture and the rise of individual (as opposed to collective) spectatorship: police interference and political pressure. In her essay, Carter argues that with regard to political posters displayed on Parisian streets, the deliberate actions of police agents, including the dispersal of crowds that gathered around posters, sought to eradicate expressions of political dissent as well as to prevent the collective reading that had historically been associated with the poster. These police actions resulted from a wider perception that the city space had been dramatically transformed and potentially radicalized through the greater distribution of textual and pictorial posters during the last decades of the century. Carter maintains that the revolutionary potential of the poster—established as early as the French Revolution—and its mode of collective spectatorship made it subject to greater scrutiny, censorship, and public debate in the period after the passage of the 1881 press liberalization law. Ultimately, she finds, through an examination of archival material and contemporary press articles, the poster's mode of reception and its political message as having earned its reputation as a subversive object that required surveillance and scrutiny even after its display had been authorized under the 1881 law. In Carter's analysis, the process of surveillance, monitoring, and, above all, the dispersal of crowds around posters by the police led to the decline of the political force of the fin-de-siècle poster.

In the final essay of this volume, two American film historians, Kenneth Garner and Richard Abel, discuss "Regulating a Risky Business: Film, Censorship, and Public Safety in Pre-War France, 1909–1914." Garner and Abel note that studies of the French film industry's strategies of legitimation have generally focused on the gradual incorporation of "respectable" culture, including, for example, using actors from the Comédie française and adapting esteemed literary works. In the period from 1909 to 1914, however, they argue, the fledgling industry also struggled against charges by municipal authorities that its products were inimical to public safety, both in terms of the "immoral" content of films, especially those claimed to instigate juvenile violence, and the physical safety of audiences exposed to highly flammable film stock. This crisis between municipal authorities and the industry came to a head during the summer of 1912 when cinemas were closed in the cities of Lyons and Hyères (Var). By examining the industry's response to this crisis through comments in trade journals, Garner and Abel argue that the censorship issue was cast in a broader regulatory discourse of "public safety" that encompassed both the issues of moral corruptibility and physical vulnerability. In order to reassure officials, the French film industry defended itself via recourse, on the one hand, to the educational nature of films and the cultural values of new "respectable" genres, and, on the other, through a demonstrated concern for physical safety through the recognition of the skill of trained projectionists. By considering censorship within this broader regulatory framework, the authors seek to demonstrate how concerns about public safety (both moral and physical) paradoxically led to the successful legitimation of the industry in the eyes of government and municipal officials by the beginning of World War I.

Each of the essays in the volume suggests that nineteenth-century French authorities were deeply concerned about the impact of visual images upon their population, especially on the less educated and often illiterate members of that population. The result was an extraordinary amount of time and energy invested in controlling these images and, for succeeding generations, a remarkable insight into the daily fears and concerns of those who bore the burden of governing France.

ROBERT JUSTIN GOLDSTEIN

Censorship of Caricature and the Theater in Nineteenth-Century France: An Overview

On September 20, 1874, the French caricature journal *L'éclipse* declared, "One could one day write an exact history of the liberty which we enjoy during this era by writing a history of our caricatures." Similarly, during an 1880 legislative debate on caricature censure, the French deputy Robert Mitchell told his colleagues that a close examination of caricatures could be enormously revealing about governmental preferences and fears:

> Drawings which displease the government are always forbidden. Those which have gained official favor are displayed in the windows of all the bookstores, are sold in all the kiosks. This provides a valuable indicator for the attentive observer, curious for precise information on the tastes, preferences, sentiments, hates and intentions of those who have control and care over our destinies. In studying refused drawings and authorized drawings, we know exactly what the government fears and what it encourages, we have a clear revelation of its intimate thoughts.[1]

French historian Odile Krakovitch reached a similar conclusion about studying theater and censorship in nineteenth-century France, especially with regard to how the repeated implementation and cancellation of censorship helps to illuminate our knowledge of the times. Studying the massive censorship archives, she concluded, provides a "marvelous witness to the preoccupations, mentalities, reflexes, struggles, fears, consciences and knowledge of people of the century," as they document a "strange ballet, with the appearance

---

1. *Journal Officiel* (JO), June 8, 1880, 6214. Translations here and throughout are my own.

YFS 122, *Out of Sight: Political Censorship of the Visual Arts in Nineteenth-Century France,* ed. Goldstein, © 2012 by Yale University.

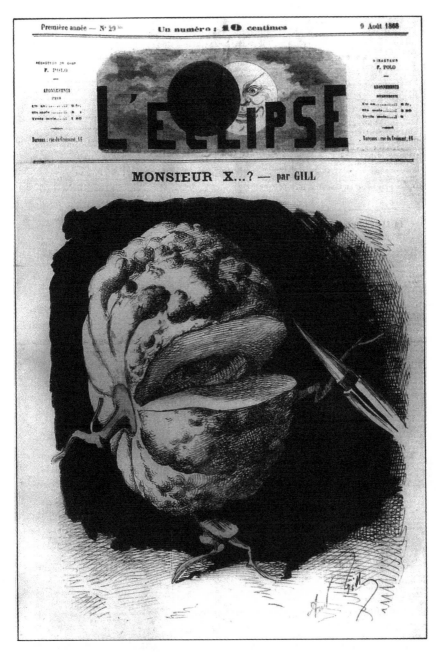

Première année — N° 29 bis   Un numéro : 10 centimes   9 Août 1868

RÉDACTEUR EN CHEF
F. POLO

ABONNEMENTS
Paris

DIRECTEUR
F. POLO

ABONNEMENTS
DÉPARTEMENTS

Bureaux : rue du Croissant, 16   Bureaux : rue du Croissant, 16

L'ECLIPSE

MONSIEUR X...? — par GILL

Figure 1. Sometimes the motives of the authorities in prosecuting caricatures remained obscure. This drawing, the famous "melon" by André Gill, which appeared in the August 9, 1868 *L'éclipse* largely became notorious because the government prosecuted Gill for "obscenity" for it. It is believed that the government thought the cantaloupe's "face" resembled that of a highly repressive judge. Gill was acquitted for the drawing and one wit quipped that the government had "descended to prosecuting vegetables." (Private collection)

and disappearance of censorship, entering and leaving at more or less regular intervals."[2]

The simultaneous study of censorship of caricature and the theater in nineteenth-century France as examples of censorship of the visual arts can be justified in many ways: both caricature and theater involved a mixture of text (caricature captions and literary scripts) and visual presentation, both tended to arouse the same fears of the authorities and, above all, both tended to be treated essentially the same by the authorities, with censorship of caricature and theater usually introduced and abolished at the same time under the same justifications. This is especially clear in 1835, when the government of King Louis Philippe successfully proposed re-introducing prior censorship of both caricature and the theater in the same laws (the so-called "September Laws") even though censorship had theoretically been abolished forever in France in the 1830 constitution adopted in the wake of the July Revolution of that year. According to French Minister of Justice Jean-Charles Persil, however, the 1830 constitutional provisions applied to censorship of the printed word only, while drama and caricature were media so different from print and so much more powerful that they could justifiably be subjected to entirely different legal treatment, including prior censorship. Thus, Persil told the French legislature that the 1830 censorship ban

> Only applies to the right to *publish* and have *printed one's opinions;* in the [written] press which is placed under the guarantee of the Constitution, it is the free manifestation of *opinions* which cannot be repressed by preventive measures. But there the solicitude of the Constitutional charter ends. It would clearly go beyond that goal if the charter were interpreted to accord the same protection to opinions converted into actions. Let an author be content to print his play, he will be subjected to no preventive measure; let the illustrator write his thought, let him publish in it that form, and as in that manner he addresses only the mind, he will encounter no obstacle. It is in that sense that it was said that censorship could never be reestablished. But when opinions are converted into *acts* by the presentation of a play or the exhibit of a drawing, one addresses people gathered together, one speaks to their eyes. That is more than the expression of

2. Odile Krakovitch, "Les ciseaux d'Anastasie: Le théâtre au XIXe siècle" in *Censures: de la Bible aux larmes d'Éros* (Paris : Éditions du centre Pompidou, 1987), 56, 63.

an opinion, that is a *deed*, an *action*, a *behavior*, with which article seven of the charter is not concerned.[3]

The parallel treatment of censorship in caricature and theater is clear not only from this argument, but also from the fact that it was often introduced and/or abolished at about the same time, usually in association with a general change of regime. Thus, prior censorship of caricature was abolished along with changes in regime in 1815, 1830, 1848 and 1870 (and for good in connection with the consolidation of the "republican republic" in 1881) and reinstated in 1820, 1835, 1852, and 1871, due either to changes in regime or, as with the September Laws, of a drastic shift in the political atmosphere. Censorship of the theater was abolished in 1830, 1848, 1870 and permanently in 1906 and re-implemented in 1835, 1850 and 1871. Although these dates are not identical they are certainly close enough to suggest, along with Persil's parallel argument, that theater and caricature were viewed quite similarly by the authorities in the threats that they were perceived as posing.

What was it about drama and drawings that made the authorities fear them so much more than writing (which we know was the case, not only because of arguments such Persil's in 1835 but, above all, because the printed word was never subject to prior censorship in France after 1822)? In short, like some other forms of visual imagery such as photographs, posters, and the cinema, which are discussed in other essays in this volume, caricature and the theater were perceived as posing a greater threat to public order and social stability than the written word because, to varying degrees, they were seen as more powerful in impact, more accessible to the lower classes (and above all the illiterate), and more likely to be viewed in a collective setting that was viewed as potentially far more inflammable than the typical private, often middle-class home in which the written word was consumed in solitude or near-solitude.

Speaking of the power and impact of drawings, the French minister of the interior told his prefects in a September 8, 1829 communication that "engravings or lithographs act immediately upon the imagination of the people, like a book which is read with the speed of light; if it wounds modesty or public decency the damage is rapid

3. *Archives parlementaires de 1787 à 1860* (AP) (Paris: Paul Ducatel, 1898), 741; emphases in original.

and irremediable." Seven years earlier, the minister of the interior warned his prefects that, "If the licensing of the press has always been a powerful auxiliary of the facts, the license of engraving is even more dangerous, because it acts directly upon the people and could lead them to revolt, or at least to scorn for the most respectable things."

Similarly, another French minister of the interior, Charles Duchatel, told the French legislature during the 1835 legislative debate on censorship of caricature that "there is nothing more dangerous, gentlemen, than these infamous caricatures, these seditious designs." They produce "the most deadly effect" and there was "no more direct provocation to crimes which we all deplore" than those posed by subversive drawings.[4] Elaborating on his basic argument that drawings and drama were entirely different media than the printed word, Justice Minister Persil maintained during the 1835 debate that it would "force the meaning of words to consider drawings the same as opinions" or to "establish a parallel between writings which address themselves to the mind and illustrations which speak to the senses" because the "vivacity and popularity of the impressions" left by caricatures created a "special danger which well-intention legislation must prevent at all costs." Legislative deputy Eugène Janvier echoed Duchatel in proclaiming that drawings "don't address opinions, they address passions" and "deprave those who observe them, degrade intelligence, address themselves only to the low chords of the heart, play with crime and frolic with assassination!"[5]

This argument that caricatures left an especially powerful impact upon public opinion is well supported by contemporary observers. Thus, in 1869 a Rouen bureaucrat informed his superiors in Paris that:

> The great Parisian newspapers play a role in the movement of public opinion, but that which dominates it especially and entertains it is the small, acrimonious press, denigrating, ironic, which freely spreads each day scorn and calumny on all that concerns the government. . . . The weekly newspapers, the illustrated [i.e. caricature] journals of opposition sell many more examples and are read much more than the serious organs of the same opinion. It is by ridicule, by perfidious jesting and defamations, that they are now making war on our institutions and the men who personify them. It is sad to avow that this

4. Archives nationales, Paris, F18 2342; AP (1898), 741.
5. AP, 741–42.

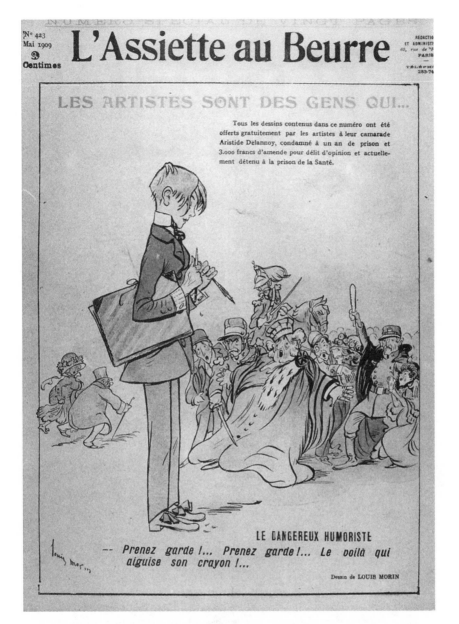

Figure 2. This May 1900 *L'assiette au beurre* caricature, by Aristide Delannoy, satirizes the fear the authorities felt about drawings. It depicts a crowd of monarchists, police, and bourgeoisie withdrawing before a caricaturist and is captioned, "The dangerous humorist. Watch Out! . . . Watch Out! He's sharpening his pencil!" Delannoy had just been prosecuted and jailed for a caricature of General d'Amade as a bloody butcher surveying the carnage he had created in the conquest of Morocco. (Private collection)

Figure 3. Caricaturists especially objected that their work was subject to prior censorship, while that of the written press was not. In this *Le grelot* drawing of December 28, 1873, entitled "It's like that," Alfred Le Petit warns that if a new press law is signed the feather pen will be just as destroyed as is caricature, which is depicted bound and gagged in the background. (Private collection)

Figure 4. In this caricature of Minister of the Interior Victor Le Franc by André Gill, from the September 19, 1872 issue of *L'éclipse*, a proud, smiling pen representing the press turns his back and Le Franc closes his right eye, while staring with his left at a bending, humiliated pencil representing the censored caricature. (Private collection)

Figure 5. In this caricature from the November 11, 1877 issue of *Le pétard*, caricaturist Alfred Le Petit shows himself tearing his hair out in frustration over caricature censorship, represented by the ugly scissor-baring Anastasie, while freedom of caricature is represented by the lack of censorship in England, demonstrated by a proud *Punch*, far left. (Private collection)

war without dignity and without good faith is succeeding among all classes.[6]

The power of caricatures was especially evident during the early 1830s, when the journals of editor Charles Philipon, *La caricature* and *Le charivari*, featured attacks on King Louis Philippe, in which the king was repeatedly depicted in the form of a pear ("poire" in French). Even the account by French historian Paul Thureau-Dangin, which is extremely hostile to Philipon, concedes that his caricatures were "perhaps even yet more dangerous" for the regime than the printed word because they had "such audacity, such importance, a power so destructive, that history cannot neglect those illustrated papers, which from other points of view it would be tempted to scorn." The English writer William Thackeray wrote that everyone who visited Paris during the 1830s "must remember the famous 'poire' which was chalked upon all the walls of the city and which bore so ludicrous a resemblance to Louis Philippe" and German author and political exile Heinrich Heine wrote that Paris was festooned with "hundreds of caricatures" hanging "everywhere" and that the "pear, and always the pear, is to be seen in every caricature" and the "glory from [the king's head] hath passed away and all men see in it is but a pear."[7]

Contemporary observers gave similar credit during the 1865–1875 period to the opposition caricatures of André Gill. Thus, historian Jules Lermina characterized the impact of his drawings during the 1860s by declaring that Gill cleverly targeted the "weak point in our political adversaries" and thus "served as one of the most useful artisans of the fall of the [Second] Empire of Napoleon III." Referring to Gill's attacks upon the so-called "monarchist republic" of the 1871–77 period, one Paris journal wrote in 1881 that Gill had "established the republic with a series of improvised masterpieces," while

6. Claude Bellanger et al., *Histoire générale de la presse française*, vol. 2 (Paris: Presses Universitaires de France, 1969), 352.

7. P. Thureau-Dangin, *Histoire de la monarchie de juillet* (Paris: Plon, 1888), 575; Charles Baudelaire, *The Painter of Modern Life*, tr. Jonathan Mayne (New York: Phaidon, 1964), 172; Heinrich Heine, *French Affairs* (New York: Heinemann, 1893), 142, 331. For extensive treatments of the "poire," see David Kerr, *Caricature and French Political Culture, 1830–1848* (Oxford: Oxford University Press, 2000); E. Kenney and J. Merriman, *The Pear: French Graphic Arts in the Golden Age of Caricature* (Mt. Holyoke, MA: Mt. Holyoke College Art Museum, 1991); Sandy Petrey, *In the Court of the Pear King: French Culture and the Rise of Realism* (Ithaca, NY: Cornell University Press, 2005); and Amy Forbes, *The Satiric Decade: Satire and the Rise of Republicanism in France, 1830–1840* (New York: Lexington Books, 2010).

a fellow caricaturist declared in 1895 that "all Republican Paris remembers that unforgettable period during which his incisive and biting pencil" struck "terrible blows against the monarchist republic."[8]

Fears and evaluations concerning the power of the stage were frequently expressed in similar terms in nineteenth-century France. Thus, even the president of the French Society of Dramatic Authors, Baron Isidore Taylor, supported censorship in testimony before an 1849 state inquiry, declaring that among all those watching, the stage produced a "sort of electric communication, even more seductive for the masses than a speech, and one thousand times more dangerous than the most vehement article in the daily press." As with caricature, the clearest evidence that such fears were widespread and directly related to the visual spectacle of the stage rather than to fear of captions or literary texts is that drama censorship was not abolished in France until 1906, while censorship of the written word ended in 1822. Theater censor Hallays-Dabot expressed ideas similar to those of Taylor in his 1862 history of theater censorship:

> An electric current runs through the playhouse, passing from actor to spectator, inflaming them both with a sudden ardor and giving them an unexpected audacity. . . . Social theories of the most false and daring nature excite an audience, who in the emotion of the drama, cannot discern the lessons from the portrayals and speeches which are presented to them. When thousands of spectators, swept along by the intoxication of the drama, are subjected to a fatal influence, when the reverberations of the scandal will create a disturbed public, what safeguard could society find in the slow and methodical march of the laws [i.e., post-production prosecution of a play]?[9]

Similarly, socialist politician Louis Blanc wrote during the 1840s in defense of stage censorship that:

> To permit a private person to act at the direction of his own caprice upon the assembled audience by the seduction of the set, the interest of the drama, the beauty of the women, the talent of the artists, the enchantment of the decoration and the lighting, that is to deliver the souls of the people as fodder to the first corrupter who comes along; that is to abandon to him the right to poison the sources of human in-

---

8. See Robert Justin Goldstein, "André Gill and the Struggle against Censorship of Caricature in France, 1867–1879," *Journalism History* 21 (1995): 143–44.

9. Krakovitch, *Les pièces de théatre soumises à la censure (1800–1830)* (Paris : Archives nationales, 1982), 14.

telligence. In such a country the government would not be worthy of the name, the state could not renounce the moral direction of society by the theater without abdicating.[10]

Aside from the feared power of their impact in general, caricature and theater were also particularly viewed with concern by the French authorities because they were accessible to the illiterate, unlike the written word. Illiteracy was not only extremely high in France, especially during the first half of the nineteenth-century, but it was especially so among the particularly feared poor "dark masses" who were viewed as unusually susceptible to revolutionary incitement. Thus, 50% of all army recruits in the 1830s were illiterate, and while fewer than 10% were illiterate by 1900, only 2% had completed secondary school. Thus, as historian Donald English has noted, throughout the century France "remained a nation of semi-literate people" for whom the image remained a "more easily understandable and accessible medium" than print.

The French police minister made his understanding of this point clear in an 1852 directive to his subordinates in which he declared that "among the means employed to shake and destroy the sentiments of reserve and morality which are so essential to conserve in the bosom of a well-ordered society, drawings are one of the most dangerous," because "the worst page of a bad book requires some time to think and a certain degree of intelligence to understand, while the drawing

10. Krakovitch, *Hugo censuré: la liberté au théâtre au XIXe siècle* (Paris : Calmann-Lévy, 1985), 83. Krakovitch's work is the best overall summary of nineteenth-century French theater censorship. For an extended English-language summary, see Goldstein, "France," in *The Frightful Stage: Political Censorship of the Theater in Nineteenth-Century Europe* , ed. Goldstein (New York: Berghahn Books, 2009), 70–129. For a summary of nineteenth-century French caricature censorship, see Goldstein, *Political Censorship of Caricature in Nineteenth-Century France* (Kent, OH: Kent State University Press, 1989). For a recent French book on the subject, see Jean-Michel Renault, *Censure et caricatures: Les images interdites et le combat de l'histoire de la Presse en France et dans le monde* (Montpellier : Pat à Pan, 2006). Comparable recent studies on theater and caricature censorship in other European countries, at least in English, are almost completely lacking, but for two extremely good exceptions to this rule, see Gary Stark, *Banned in Berlin: Literary Censorship in Imperial Germany, 1871–1918* (New York: Berghahn Books, 2009); and David King and Cathy Porter, *Images of Revoluion: Graphic Art from 1905 Russia* (New York: Random House, 1983). For overall summaries of nineteenth-century European (including press) censorship, see Goldstein, *Political Censorship of the Arts and the Press in Nineteenth-Century Europe* (New York: Palgrave Macmillan, 1989), based primarily on English-language sources; and *The War for the Public Mind: Political Censorship in Nineteenth Century Europe*, ed. Goldstein (Westport, CT: Praeger Publishers, 2000).

communicates with movement and life, as to thus present spontane-
ously, in a translation which everyone can understand, the most dangerous of all seductions, that of example." This not-so-subtle reference to the ability of drawings to communicate with "everyone" (i.e.,
even the poorly educated and illiterate) was made even clearer during an 1880 legislative debate on caricature censorship, when deputy
Emile Villiers declared that while press freedom posed "problems and
dangers," the "unlimited freedom of drawings presents many more
still," since a drawing "startles not only the mind but the eyes" and
was a means of speaking "even to the illiterate, of stirring up passions,
without reasoning, without discourse." The special dangers posed by
making seditious drawings available to the poor and illiterate were
also made clear in an 1829 interior ministry directive, in which the
French prefects were informed that "in general, that which can be
permitted with difficulty when it is a question of expensive illustrations, or lithographs intended only to illustrate an important [i.e.,
expensive] work would be dangerous and must be forbidden when
these same subjects are reproduced in engravings and lithographs at
a cheap price."[11]

The same fear about the accessibility of drawings to the illiterate
was clearly also a factor in the view of French officials about the special dangers posed by the stage. Thus, at a time when the theater was
widely considered to be the most important venue for the education
of the lower classes, theater inspectors during the reign of King Louis
Philippe were directed to report in great detail about what they observed in theaters "in which the coarsest classes of people gather,"
since such venues had become "the only school in which the lower
class of society goes to learn its lessons." Not only was French theater censorship implemented far after censorship of the written press
was abolished, but such fears about the impact of the stage upon the
illiterate were reflected in the fact that theater material viewed as
specifically targeting the "dark masses" was typically subjected to
particularly strict controls. As John House notes in a study of French
censorship of images during the 1860s, while the authorities were in
general "particularly wary of the potency of visual experience in the
form of a print or a stage representation or a performance of a popular

---

11. Donald English, *Political Uses of Photography in the Third French Republic,
1871–1914* (Ann Arbor, MI: UMI Research Press, 1984), 16; AN F18 2342; JO, June 8,
1880, 6212–13.

café concert song," the "question of class—of determining what types of materials should be permitted for which social groups—seems to have been the most fundamental concern."[12]

As a result, the severity of the French theater censorship partly depended upon the perceived class nature of the intended audience, and as Krakovitch sums up, "The more modest and popular the theater the harsher the censors' judgments and the more numerous the required modifications." Thus, plays that were approved for "legitimate" state-sponsored theaters typically patronized by the upper and middle classes were often barred from the popular stage. *La mort en loterie*, for example, intended for the popular Gaité, was banned because, according to the censors, "if reform ideas which attack one of our penal institutions are admissible in the sphere of politics and philosophy, they are out of place in a vaudeville intended for a Boulevard [popular] theater." Similarly, during Napoleon III's reign, a censor wrote, concerning King Lear, that "its boldness could only be presented in an essentially literary venue, before an elite public" and "before the public of the Boulevard it would be a spectacle whose philosophical import would not be understood but in which we fear only the degradation of royalty would be perceived."[13]

Until 1864, to further ensure that the theater would present only "safe" dramas to lower classes, all theater owners had to undergo police scrutiny to receive licenses and to post sometimes extremely heavy bonds to be forfeited in case of legal violations. Thus, the director of Paris's Vaudeville Theater had to deposit a bond 300,000 francs in 1864, the staggering equivalent of $60,000 in American money of the time (similar so-called caution or security bonds were required for publishers of caricature journals and other newspapers, thus ensuring that poor people could not be theater or editorial directors). Before the 1864 termination of the theater licensing requirements, theoretically only the handful of state-subsidized theaters could perform so-called "legitimate" stage presentations, such as "serious" comedies, tragedies, and operas, while the popular "Boulevard" theaters could

12. John House, "Manet's Maximilian: Censorship and the Salon," in *Suspended License: Censorship and the Visual Arts*, ed. Elizabeth Childs (Seattle, WA: University of Washington Press, 1997), 18.

13. Krakovitch, "Robert Macaire ou la grande peur des censeurs," *Europe: Revue litteraire mensuelle* 65 (1987) : 55–56; Jean-Marie Thomasseasu, "Le mélodrame et la censure sous le Premier Empire et la Restauration," *Revue des sciences humaines* 162 (1976) : 179; Krakovitch, *Hugo*, 114, 131, 140.

officially present only pantomimes, vaudevilles, short skits and songs that were unlikely to encompass serious political critiques. Yet censorship of French café-concerts was especially harsh due to their heavily working class audience during the late nineteenth-century, with about 10% of all songs proposed for such venues banned, a percentage far exceeding that for plays.[14]

As mentioned above, the French authorities also especially feared drawings and the theater because they posed the particular danger of attracting a collective audience that might be incited to immediate disorder, unlike reading, which was typically conducted in the privacy of a (preferably middle class) home. This was, of course, especially true with regard to the theater, which largely explains why theater censorship extended until 1906 while caricature censorship was abolished in 1881. Theater by definition was consumed collectively, but many caricatures, which took on the character of large posters when displayed in shop windows, kiosks, and newsstands, also attracted a collective audience, as is evidenced by many surviving caricatures that themselves depict the crowds examining them. Thus, one of the famous "poire" caricatures (from Philipon's *La caricature* of December 22, 1831) portrays a crowd of people examining caricatures displayed at the office of his printer, Aubert, near the Palais Royale, while one man faces the reader and proclaims, "You have to admit the head of government looks awfully funny." Fears of the impact of theater upon its always collective audience were naturally even stronger than were fears of the immediate impact of a perceived dangerous caricature: one French prison director even proclaimed, "When they put on a bad drama, a number of young new criminals soon arrive at my prison." Throughout the nineteenth century, advocates of theater censorship cited the widespread (but highly exaggerated) belief that the Dutch opera *La Muette de Portici* had triggered the successful 1830 Belgian revolution against Dutch rule, while the French theater censor Victor Hallays-Dabat wrote in 1862 that several plays presented in the 1840s had effectively provided a "sort of dress rehearsal" for the 1848 revolution. Thus, Hallays-Dabat wrote, "The public is like a group of children. Each of them by themselves is sweet, innocuous, sometimes fearful; but bring them together and

---

14. Concetta Condemi, *Les café-concerts* (Paris : Quai Voltaire, 1992), 39; Eva Kimminich, "Chansons étouffée: Recherche sur le café-concert au XIX siècle," *Politix* 4 (1991) : 19–26.

Notre Gérant chez Mme Anastasie

Figure 6. Caricaturists' hatred of censorship is shown once again in this drawing from the June 25, 1881 issue of *La trique*, in which a censorship-pearl is wasted on the swine of the censor Anastasie. (Courtesy, University of Wisconsin Library)

you are faced with a group that is bold and noisy, often wicked. The courage or rather the cowardice of anonymity is such a powerful force!"[15]

The goals of the French theater and caricature censorship were always clear, even if specific guidelines were sometime vaguely stated: the protection of the existing political, social, economic, and moral order. Thus, according to an analysis of over 200 censorship and prosecutorial decisions involving plays, newspapers, and novels undertaken by four different French regimes between 1815 and 1870, about 55% of all such actions were based on perceived challenges to existing political and social authorities, with the balance almost all involving offense to the "moral" order. Officials during the Second Republic and Second Empire directed the drama censors to specifically eliminate "attacks against the principle of authority, against religion, the family, the courts, the army, in a word against the institutions upon which society rests" and especially to ban all scenes imbued with a "revolutionary spirit" or that presented "social ideas" or inspired "class antagonism," as well as "all forms of factionalism, based on the principles that the theater must be a place of repose and of distraction and not an overt arena of political passions."[16] Among the specific examples reflecting such principles effected by the theater censorship, Victor Hugo's *Marion de Lorme* was banned because it unfavorably depicted Charles X's long-dead ancestor Louis XIII and Alfred de Musset's 1861 *Lorenzaccio*, a play about Renaissance Italy, was forbidden on the grounds, as the censors put it, that, "The discussion of the right to assassinate a sovereign whose crimes and iniquities, even including the murder of the prince by his parents, cry out for vengeance . . . is a dangerous spectacle to present to the public." Similar sensitivities led to frequent bans on materials that were seen as mocking even low-level governmental officials or inciting class conflict. Thus, censors refused to allow the phrase "the rich, in the design of God, are only the treasurers of the poor" from an 1853 play, and banned from Victor Séjour's 1860 *Les aventuriers* the comment

15. Cahuet, 348; Sonia Slatin, "Opera and Revolution: *Muette de Portici* and the Belgian Revolution of 1830 Revisited," *Journal of Musicological Research* 3 (1979): 45–62; Hallays-Dabot, 116.

16. Krakovitch, *Hugo*, 150, 244–45, 227, 286; Cahuet, 206, 217; James Allen, *In the Public Eye: A History of Reading in Modern France* (Princeton, NJ: Princeton University Press, 1991), 94; AN F18 2342, 2363.

that, "If a rich man wants to go hunting or dancing they rollout a carpet for him lest he weary his feet."[17]

Altogether, during the 1835–1847 period, of a total of 8,330 plays submitted to the French censorship, 219 (2.6%) were completely banned and another 488 (5.6%) underwent enforced modifications. During the especially ferocious censorship that followed Napoleon III's 1851 coup d'état, of 682 submitted plays reported on in 1853, only 246 were approved intact, while 59 (8.4%) were rejected outright and changes were demanded in another 323 (47.4%). About 40 plays were banned in the aftermath of the 1871 Commune between 1870 and 1874, although thereafter theater interdictions became quite rare, with only about 20 plays banned between 1874 and the end of theater censorship in 1906 (including Zola's famous *Germinal* and Sardou's *Thermidor*, the first being anathema to the Left and the second, to the Right).[18]

The censors rejected and/or prosecuted thousands of caricatures between 1820 and 1881, including over 200 each in several years, including 1864, 1875, 1877 and 1880. In 1875, one liberal Republican caricature journal, *Le grelot*, suffered 67 censorship rejections under the rule of the "monarchist republic," while in 1880 under a moderate Republican regime, the monarchist caricature journal *Le Triboulet* suffered 42 caricature bans. The most common themes expressed in attacks on caricatures were that they denigrated government officials, created disrespect for the established order, demoralized society, often bordered on obscenity, and even played at revolution and/or assassination. Thus, during the 1835 legislative debate on censorship of caricature, the duc de Broglie, King Louis Philippe's prime minister, referred to caricatures as a display of "disgusting obscenities, of infamous baseness, of dirty productions" that forced pedestrians to "lower our eyes blushing from shame." During the trial of the caricature journal *Le charivari* in April 1835, the government prosecutor declared that "before overthrowing a regime, one undermines it by sarcasm, one casts scorn upon it."[19]

17. Krakokvich, *Hugo*, 15, 240; W. D. Howart, *Sublime and Grotesque: A Study of French Romantic Drama* (London: Harrap, 1975), 306; Charles O'Neill, "Theatrical Censorship in France, 1844–1875: The Experience of Victor Séjour,' *Harvard Library Bulletin* 26 (1878): 434.

18. Krakovitch, *Hugo*, 224, 248–49, 286–87; Josette Parrain, "Censure, théâtre et commune, 1871–1914," *Mouvement Social* 79 (1972) : 327–42.

19. Goldstein, *Censorship*, 5, 6, 12.

Although specific guidelines for the caricature censors were rare, they were generally quite similar to those provided to the theater censors. Thus, an 1822 dispatch from the minister of the interior to the prefects urged them to examine with "particular care" all illustrations that could present some character of immorality, irreligion, or outrage upon the king," and an 1879 document directed the censors to refuse "absolutely" drawings that were directed "against the head of state" and to authorize only "with the greatest circumspection concerning the legislative chambers, the magistrates, the army, religion or the clergy." According to 1829 guidelines from the minister of the interior, religion must be protected "from all direct or indirect offense, including all fiction or allusion which could wound it," and no attacks could be made upon "legitimate authority," including those that subjected the "royal majesty and the august dynasty of the Bourbons" to "attacks or allusions of whatever kind," as well as similar attacks upon "foreign monarchs," as the "sovereigns are reciprocal support of one another with regard to all which could attack their sacred character."[20] Perhaps two of the most famous caricatures that ran into censorship trouble in nineteenth-century France portrayed French monarchs extremely unfavorably. Daumier's 1831 "Gargantua," depicting King Louis Philippe as sitting on a toilet throne excreting boodle to his courtiers while extracting graft from the poor people of France led to a six-month jail term during a period when prior censorship of caricature was not in effect, while Gill's 1867 "Rocambole," which snuck by the censors with its portrayal of Emperor Napoleon III as a half-dandy, half-bandit, eventually led to the banning of *La lune*, the journal in which it appeared. Altogether, between 1815 and 1880 about 20 French caricature journals were banned by the government and virtually every prominent nineteenth-century French political caricaturist had his drawings forbidden, was prosecuted and/or jailed.[21]

20. Goldstein, *Censorship*, 11–12.
21. Goldstein, *Censorship*, 11–12; Elizabeth Childs, "Big Trouble: Daumier, Gargantua, and the Censorship of Political Caricature," *Art Journal* 51 (1992), 26–37. See also Childs, "The Body Impolitic: Censorship and the Caricature of Honoré Daumier," in Childs, *Suspended*, 148–85.

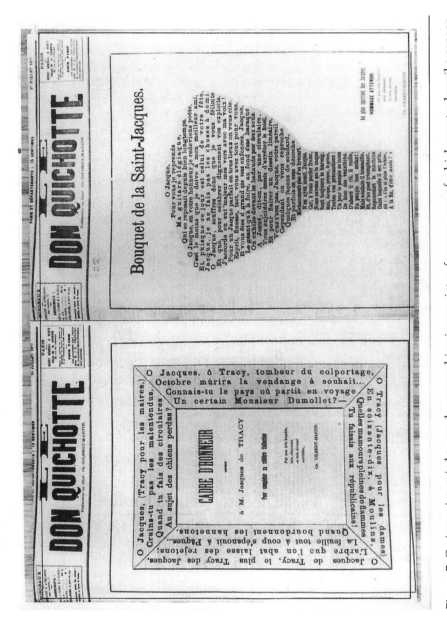

Figure 7. Caricaturists tried to evade censorship via a variety of means, one of which was to describe censorship in words or designs, as in the July 20 and July 27, 1877 issues of *Le Don Quichotte* shown here. Both make reference in their titles to the local censor Jacques de Tracy. (Courtesy Wayne State University Library)

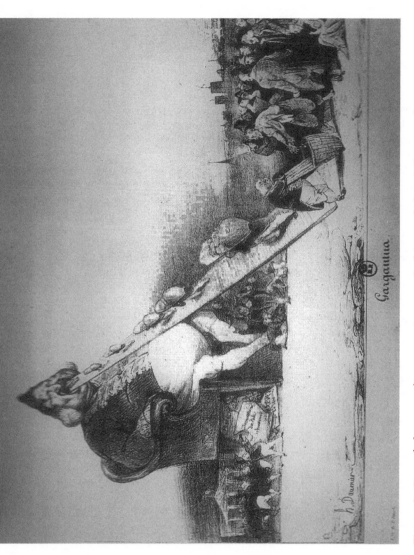

Figrue 8. One of the most famous caricatures in history led to jail terms for artist Honoré Daumier. Entitled "Gargantua," it depicted King Louis-Phillipe sitting on a toilet-throne, inhaling graft and boodle from the poor people of France and excreting graft to upper classes, far left. (Published as a separate print December 1831, courtesy Bibliothèque Nationale, Paris.)

Figure 9. In this famous caricature, "Authentic Portrait of Rocambole," published in the November 17, 1867 *La lune*, André Gill depicts Emperor Napoleon III as half-bandit and half-dandy, as can be seen if a line is drawn vertically through the emperor's face. Although this picture slipped through the censorship, *La lune* was soon closed down (and replaced by *L'éclipse*). (Courtesy University of Connecticut Library)

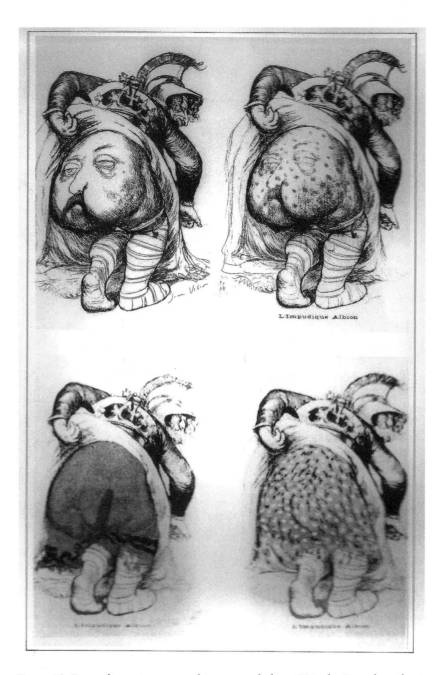

L'Impudique Albion

Figure 10. Even after prior censorship was ended in 1881, the French authorities maintained the right to ban street sales of individual caricatures. This caricature, entitled "Impudent Albion" was made famous by such a street sale. It shows British King Edward VII on the bare bottom of a soldier; when the authorities banned it, the September 28, 1901 issue of *L'assiette au beurre* in which it first appeared reprinted the caricature, each time covering up slightly more of the king's features.

DAVID O'BRIEN

Censorship of Visual Culture in France, 1815–1852

Systematic censorship of visual culture in France was confined largely to print media. Fernand Drujon's still-useful catalogue of objects proscribed by the French government between 1814 and 1877 begins with a section devoted to the censorship of "emblems and objects of a diverse nature" before turning to books, newspapers, pamphlets, and prints. His list is short and primarily devoted to instances from the 1870s. For the period that concerns us here, from 1815 to 1852, Drujon cites only a handful of examples. In 1823 police seized busts of the Duke of Reichstadt, the son of Napoleon and Marie-Louise and heir to the Napoleonic throne. In 1829, officials confiscated scarves decorated with the effigy of the very same duke and prosecuted the merchant selling them. In 1830, after the revolution of that year, the government suppressed coins bearing the likeness of the would-be Henri V, son of Charles X and pretender to the Bourbon throne. Police seized some fifty packets of damask handkerchiefs decorated with fleurs de lis, the image of the Duke of Bordeaux (i.e., Henri V), and a verse claiming his legal right to the throne in 1838. Two prosecutions for plaster medallions with unspecified images took place in 1851. Finally, in the same year one Prosper Vassal was imprisoned for selling a "white clay pipe representing a nude woman letting show, under her skirts, her sexual parts, colored red."[1]

Drujon admitted that his list was very incomplete and remarked that "no one in the years that have just passed" could have failed to

1. Fernand Drujon, *Catalogue des ouvrages, écrits et dessins poursuivis, supprimés ou condamnés depuis le 21 octobre 1814 jusqu'au 31 juillet 1877*, édition entièrement nouvelle (Paris: Edouard Rouveyre, 1879), xxii-xxxv. I wish to thank Robert Goldstein, Sheryl Kroen, Catherine Chevillot, Ségolène Le Men, and Claire Barbillon for their generous help in the preparation of this article. Translations throughout are my own.

YFS 122, *Out of Sight: Political Censorship of the Visual Arts in Nineteenth-Century France*, ed. Goldstein, © 2012 by Yale University.

notice the sale of licentious statuettes and match cases and tobacco jars representing political figures. "Indeed, one of the objects that you encounter most frequently is the Republic wearing a Phrygian cap painted red, which serves as a lid." However, he concluded, "Convictions specifically motivated by the sale of these sorts of objects are extremely rare."[2] This essay reexamines the censorship of visual culture, setting aside for the most part printed images as their case is sufficiently complex to merit separate treatment in this volume. Censorship on non-print objects was more widespread than Drujon suspected, but more importantly, it varied enormously across different types of visual culture, revealing much about its preoccupations and goals.

A number of recent cultural histories that touch on the subject of censorship reveal the incompleteness of Drujon's list. Sheryl Kroen finds that during the Restoration police confiscated a whole array of objects—candy boxes, tobacco cases, wine labels, chairs, neckties, swimsuits, hats, suspenders—and sometimes punished their owners. Often these objects carried illustrations of politically objectionable figures, but sometimes simply a reference to the colors of the Republican flag was enough to have them censored.[3] Barbara Day-Hickman has highlighted the large amount of Napoleonic paraphernalia that survives from the Restoration despite the ban on such objects. For the wealthy there existed:

> jewelry, silverware, fans, and lamps that replicated characteristic portraits of Bonaparte. The middle classes purchased bronze statues, clocks, and expensive engravings of Napoleon to display privately in their homes, while less-monied customers in rural areas acquired suspenders, kerchiefs, pipes, and wood-block images of the Little Corporal from itinerant peddlers.[4]

A painting of a peddler of plaster figurines from just after the Restoration helps us to imagine how the lower end of this market might have looked (fig. 1). As Day-Hickman observes, this list indicates that Napoleon had broad appeal across social classes. Significantly, the government seemed primarily concerned with objects directed

2. Ibid., xxxv.
3. Sheryl Kroen, *Poltics and Theater: The Crisis of Legitimacy in Restoration France, 1815–1830* (Berkeley: University of California Press, 2000), 191–93.
4. Barbara Ann Day-Hickman, *Napoleonic Art: Nationalism and the Spirit of Rebellion in France (1815–1848)* (Newark: University of Delaware Press, 1999), 18.

Figure 1. Joseph-Louis-Hippolyte Bellange (1800–1866), "The Plaster Merchant," 1833. Oil on canvas, 81 x 100 cm. D1975.123. Musée des Civilisations de l'Europe et de la Méditerranée, Paris, France. Photo credit : Réunion des Musées Nationaux/Art Resource, NY.

at the lower classes. In reports that the Minister of the Interior Jules Polignac wrote about these objects, he noted their ubiquity and that many were luxury items, but he expressed the opinion that the law banning them should be enforced particularly with regard to objects intended for "the less educated classes."[5] Here as elsewhere, it is clear that official censorship was especially concerned with controlling the opinion of the masses.

Other studies make clear that censorship of everyday objects continued throughout the period under a variety of pretexts. In 1841, for example, the government censored a statuette entitled *La Marseillaise* that carried the inscription "Aux armes citoyens! 1789 et 1830" and depicted a worker standing on broken chains and raising a rifle in the air.[6] In 1849 the Prefect of the Rhône praised a mayor for having "banished the *bonnet rouge*" from his town.[7] In 1850 the Procurer General in Dijon sent the police to whitewash the walls of a café in a nearby village: "On the walls could be seen pictures portraying various figures, the man of the people, the *sans-culotte* dressed in the red cap, and a woman dripping blood from her breasts who stands for the regeneration of 1793."[8]

Censorship even extended into the plant kingdom. Liberty trees were planted after each of the major revolutions of the nineteenth century and then assiduously cut down, often only a short time later. In the Drôme a prefect had a liberty tree cut down in 1816, and in 1831 his successor ordered the destruction of all the liberty trees that had been planted the previous year. A new crop of liberty trees took root in 1848, but in 1851 the national government had them felled.[9] Another example from 1851 is particularly suggestive: in the Vaucluse, prohibited from singing Republican songs, peasants took to wearing sprigs of thyme (or *la farigoulas*, a common native plant) and singing "We will plant thyme, it will take root, and the Mountain will flower."[10] The emblem in question here—a ubiquitous, naturally

5. Ibid., 34.

6. Michael Paul Driskel, "Singing 'the Marseillaise' in 1840: The Case of Charlet's Censored Prints," *Art Bulletin* 69/1 (December, 1987): 614.

7. T.J. Clark, *The Absolute Bourgeois: Artists and Politics in France, 1848–1851* (Berkeley: University of California Press, 1973), 56.

8. Cited from T.J. Clark, *The Image of the People: Gustave Courbet and the 1848 Revolution* (Berkeley: University of California Press, 1973), 94.

9. Olivier Ihl, *La fête républicaine* (Paris, 1996), 242–50.

10. Philippe Vigier, *La Seconde République dans la région alpine. Étude politique et sociale* (Paris: Presses Universitaires de France, 1963), vol. II, 267.

occurring plant—seems chosen in part to imply the futility of censorship and the irrepressibility of Republican ideas. It also points to the ease with which any aspect of visual culture might take on political meaning. As Drujon noted, Napoleon III's decree of 17 February 1852, which permitted the suppression of political signs, led to increased censorship of all sorts of objects because, as he explained, "everything . . . is susceptible to being chosen as an emblem."[11]

Flags were perhaps the most censored of non-printed objects. In 1816 the Restoration ordered the destruction of tricolor flags and other "proscribed signs," and *mairies* and prefectures around France organized ceremonies to burn flags and emblems of the Republic and Empire.[12] The Charter of 1830 returned France to "her colors" and instituted new restrictions by authorizing only tricolor cockades at festivals and political events.[13] Both red flags (the sign of the radical Left) and white flags (the sign of legitimists) were frequently suppressed at public events from 1830 onwards. For example, during the Republican insurrection occasioned by the funeral of General Jean Maximilien Lamarque in 1832, a young draughtsman named Michel-Ange Geoffroy was caught with a red flag and charged with "having displayed, in a public place, a sign or symbol intended to spread the spirit of rebellion and trouble the public peace," while another man was convicted of "having publicly carried an exterior rallying sign not authorized by the king or police regulations."[14] Rémi Dalisson reports a number of instances from the July Monarchy where local officials prohibited flags and other political symbols at festivals.[15]

The Second Republic continued these policies, making the tricolor flag "the only emblem authorized at public festivals," though allowances were made for a red rosette on the flagpole.[16] In 1848, Marc Caussidière, the Prefect of Police for the Provisional Government, informed the commissioners of each department: "The red flag

11. Ibid., xxiv.
12. Rémi Dalisson, *Les trois couleurs, Marianne et l'Empereur. Fêtes libérales et politiques symboliques en France 1815–1870* (Paris: La Boutique de l'Histoire, 2004), 19.
13. Ibid., 68.
14. Maurice Dommanget, *Histoire du drapeau rouge des origines à la guerre de 1939* (Paris: Éditions Librairie de l'Étoile, 1967), 51, 54. See also Gabriel Perreux, *Les origines du drapeau rouge en France* (Paris: Presses universitaires de France, 1930), 35–36.
15. Dalisson, 131–32.
16. Ibid., 145

is a call to insurrection, the red cap [Phrygian cap] raises memories of blood and mourning. Bearing these sad emblems provokes violence and disobedience to the law."[17] This suggests it was less through direct censorship than through other laws (against inciting violence or disobedience of the law) that people were dissuaded from carrying certain political emblems, but direct censorship did occur. Maurice Dommanget notes that one Jean Bousquet, a barista from Moissac, was tried and acquitted in 1849 in Montauban for "the public exhibition of red caps and flags."[18] Others were tried for speaking in favor of the red flag or claiming that it was the true flag of the Republic.[19]

These various examples suggest that a systematic search in archives and newspapers would uncover many more instances of censorship of everyday objects transformed into political signs. Taken together, they seem to indicate that local or low-level officials censored a great many objects, relying on a variety of laws and regulations that were not primarily intended for this purpose. Indeed, little effort seems to have been made on the national level to enforce their proscription. Furthermore, the confiscation and destruction of objects, or the prosecution of individuals for their possession, took place more or less continuously during this period and across all of France.

In contrast, more aesthetically prestigious objects such as paintings and sculptures were closely controlled by the national government, but their relation to standard modes of censorship was complex. Censorship policies varied according to an art form's relative reliance on state support or financial self-sufficiency. In contrast to popular modes of cultural production such as theater and publishing, art forms that depended heavily on the state for the costs of creation or display, such as opera and large-scale painting and sculpture, could be controlled from behind the scenes through patronage, pensions, and honors, obviating the need for overt, punitive, or *ex post facto*

17. Dommanget, *La Révolution de 1848 et le drapeau rouge* (Paris: Spartacus, n.d.), 55–56.

18. Ibid., 70.

19. Ibid., 70–71. For more on flags, see also Jean-Paul Garnier, *Le drapeau blanc* (Paris: Perrin, 1971); Georges Virenque, *Nos couleurs nationales* (Tours: Maison Alfred Mame et fils, n.d.); Arthur Maury, *Les emblèmes et les drapeaux de la France. Le coq gaulois* (Paris: no publisher, c. 1904); Dario Gamboni, *The Destruction of Art: Iconoclasm and Vandalism since the French Revolution* (New Haven: Yale University Press, 1997); and Raoul Girardet, "Les trois couleurs," in *Les lieux de mémoires*, ed. Pierre Nora (Paris: Gallimard, 1984), 5–35.

methods.[20] Control of museums provided the government with one opportunity to display or hide works of art. The Restoration, for example, removed all paintings celebrating Napoleon from the walls of the Luxembourg and Louvre museums. Major canvases by Jacques-Louis David, Antoine-Jean Gros, Anne-Louis Girodet, François Gérard, and many others disappeared from view. Louis-Philippe's regime proved more lenient, allowing for the display of most older paintings of interest, but it still censored works. For example, Eugène Delacroix's *Liberty Guiding the People*, though purchased by the government in 1831, was quickly relegated to storage, much to the artist's chagrin.[21]

The most direct state control over art came through patronage (most large-scale paintings were commissioned by the government) and control of the Salon, a government-sponsored exhibition held annually or biennially in the Louvre. A jury controlled admission into the Salon, and simply the knowledge that such a barrier existed ensured that few would attempt to enter a politically unacceptable work. There were exceptions. Most famously, Théodore Géricault created an enormous canvas for the Salon in 1819 depicting the survivors of the shipwreck of the Medusa, who were marooned on a raft for thirteen days. The painting was an unambiguous indictment of government policy, for the incompetent captain of the ship was an aristocrat and former émigré who had received his post as a result of favoritism. Géricault was forced to change the title of his painting from *The Raft of the Medusa* to *A Scene from a Shipwreck*, but the work was exhibited.[22] Others were less fortunate, and political considerations played a key role in some jury decisions during the Restoration.[23] For instance, Horace Vernet had two paintings rejected,

20. David O'Brien, *After the Revolution: Antoine-Jean Gros, Painting and Propaganda Under Napoleon* (University Park: Pennsylvania State Press, 2006), 171–73.

21. Arlette Sérullaz and Vincent Pomarède, *Eugène Delacroix*. "La Liberté guidant le peuple" (Paris: Réunion des musées nationaux, 2004), 56–57.

22. The literature on the painting is vast, but for recent analyses of its political aspects, see the essays by Bruno Chenique in Musée des Beaux-Arts de Lyon, *Géricault. La folie d'un monde* (Paris: Hazan, 2006). Geneviève and Jean Lacambre note that the work was clearly intended for purchase by a museum, but the administration decided not to buy it. See Geneviève and Jean Lacambre, "La politique d'acquisition sous la Restauration: les tableaux d'histoire," *Bulletin de la Société de l'Histoire de l'Art français*, année 1972 (1973): 334.

23. For overviews of Restoration policies see William Hauptman, "Juries, Protests, and Counter-Exhibitions Before 1850," *Art Bulletin* 67/1 (March, 1985): 95–109; Marie-

The Battle of Jemappes and *The Barrière de Clichy*, from the Salon of 1822. The first represented one of the inaugural battles of the Revolutionary wars; the second depicted a scene from the defense of Paris at the fall of the Empire in 1814. Upon their rejection, Vernet decided to exhibit forty-five paintings in his own studio, to which the government voiced no objection.[24] Significantly, both Géricault and Vernet possessed sizable personal fortunes, permitting them to pursue their projects despite government hostility. Few artists had comparable means, and thus large-scale painting's reliance on official patronage rendered overt censorship largely unnecessary.

The government's laissez-faire attitude toward Vernet's exhibition reflects a general tolerance of independent artistic exhibitions that remained true throughout the period from 1815 to 1852. Solo and group exhibitions of art occurred sporadically from the Revolution onwards, in direct contrast to what was permitted under the Old Regime. Sometimes these had themes critical of government policy, as was the case for a series of exhibitions in support of the Greek War of Independence held in 1826.[25] Nevertheless, the Salon remained the primary venue, and the state the primary patron, for large-scale painting.[26]

The July Monarchy made a show of its liberalism regarding the Salon, radically reorganizing the composition of the jury and accepting work from a broad range of political and aesthetic points of view. There were, however, artists who may well have suffered for their political affiliations (as has been suggested for the sculptor August Préault and the painters Philippe-Auguste Jeanron and Paul Chenavard). Michael Marrinan has demonstrated that in the first decade of Louis-Philippe's rule the Salon jury censored pictures dealing with the more gruesome aspects of the Terror, perhaps sometimes working upon orders from above.[27] In 1837, following Louis-Napoleon

---

Claude Chaudonneret, *L'État et les artistes. De la Restauration à la monarchie de Juillet (1815–1833)* (Paris: Flammarion, 1999); and Geneviève and Jean Lacambre, 330–344.

24. The most recent and accurate account of the Vernet episode is in Chaudonneret, 102–108. See also J. Ruutz Rees, *Horace Vernet* (New York: Scribner and Welford, 1880), 7–10.

25. Valérie Bajou, "Les expositions de la galerie Lebrun en 1826," in Réunion des musées nationaux, *La Grèce en révolte. Delacroix et les peintres français 1815–1848* (Paris: Réunion des musées nationaux, 1996), 51–58.

26. For an excellent summary on art exhibitions other than the Salon in this period, see Hauptman.

27. Michael Marrinan, *Painting Politics for Louis-Philippe: Art and Ideology in Orleanist France, 1830–1848* (New Haven: Yale University Press, 1988), 125–33.

Bonaparte's failed coup attempt, a picture by Joseph Beaume of Napoleon departing from Elba was eliminated from the Salon, despite the
fact that the government itself had commissioned the painting the
previous year.[28] On the whole, however, juries seem to have based
their decisions largely on aesthetic criteria, and they were at times
more exclusive or less so. The Second Republic proved to be excep-
tionally liberal in regard to the Salon, abolishing the jury in 1848 and
appointing a very lenient, elected jury in 1849. Instances of political
censorship of paintings at public exhibitions continued right up until
World War II, but in relation to other domains of visual culture, these
efforts seem modest at best.[29]

The contrast between the fate of painting and that of prints is revealing. All regimes during the period under consideration began by
abolishing censorship of prints, but all soon reinstituted an office ded-
icated to censoring them prior to publication.[30] Between September
1835 and February 1848 this bureau rejected over 430 drawings.[31] The
special attention received by print culture is further demonstrated by
the fact that between 1849 and 1852, 3,100 colporteurs were convicted
of selling unapproved printed materials, many of which were images.[32] Yet not all prints were considered equally. Without question, political caricatures and pornographic images were the primary target of
censors, yet if we look beyond these types of images, other priorities
in government censorship emerge.[33] Cheap woodblock prints were in
general far more policed than images with higher artistic ambitions.
For example, the Pellerin firm, which produced crude, inexpensive
woodblock prints in the town of Épinal, was more or less continuously
harassed by authorities during the Restoration for producing images

28. Ibid., 176–77.

29. For the period from 1850 to 1914, see Bernard Tillier's essay in this volume.

30. For censorship of political caricature and prints, see Robert Justin Goldstein,
"France," in *The War for the Public Mind: Political Censorship in Nineteenth-Century
Europe*, ed. Goldstein (Westport, CN: Praeger, 2000), 125–74; idem, *Political Censor-
ship of the Arts and the Press in Nineteenth-Century Europe* (New York: St. Martin's,
1989); and Elizabeth C. Childs, "The Body Impolitic: Censorship and the Caricature of
Honoré Daumier," in *Suspended License: Censorship and the Visual Arts*, ed. Childs
(Seattle: University of Washington Press, 1997), 148–84.

31. Goldstein, *Censorship of Political Caricature in Nineteenth-Century France*,
155.

32. Goldstein, "France," 148.

33. The priority given to political caricature and pornography is apparent in
the lists of censored prints in Drujon and *Catalogue des écrits, gravures et dessins
condamnés depuis 1814 jusqu'au 1er janvier 1850* (Paris: Pillet fils aîné, 1850).

of Napoleon, and Jean-Charles Pellerin was imprisoned in 1817. Yet in the same period Géricault, Horace Vernet, and Nicolas-Toussaint Charlet churned out lithographs of Napoleonic battle scenes essentially unperturbed by government officials. Whereas Pellerin aimed his folksy images at the broadest possible market, Vernet and Charlet appealed to an artistically minded and relatively wealthier audience. Pellerin's conviction specifically mentioned that his prints raised "false hopes among the common people."[34] In 1829 the government refused to grant his son permission to publish a Napoleonic print, stating that "this image may be sold in large volume among a widespread lower-class population because of its low cost."[35] Under the July Monarchy, Charlet would become the most censored artist in France, but this was only after he had become the nation's most popular graphic artist and lithography had firmly established itself as the medium of political caricature.[36]

Thus, the cultural prestige of the medium and the class affiliation of its perceived audience greatly affected its treatment by the government. The case of public sculpture bears this out, but is complicated insofar as it was both an artistically prestigious medium and often exhibited to the broadest possible public. The nineteenth century's penchant for statues in public places was so pronounced as to earn it the appellation "statuomania." Still very much a budding phenomenon in the period from 1815 to 1852, it reached its apogee only under the Third Republic. The great majority of nineteenth-century statues depicted commoners from many walks of life whose achievements had made them famous (as opposed to the saints, kings, and the occasional noble that dominated pre-Revolutionary public sculpture), but monuments also depicted religious figures and scenes, political allegories and personifications, historical episodes, and more purely mythological or decorative motifs. Maurice Agulhon has seen in this cult of famous men a "liberal humanism" that promoted a secular, democratic, meritocratic, optimistic, and pedagogical vision of history.[37] More immediately, these statues were important expressions

34. Day-Hickman, 41.
35. Ibid., 46.
36. Michael Paul Driskel, "Singing 'the Marseillaise' in 1840: The Case of Charlet's Censored Prints," *Art Bulletin* 69/1 (December, 1987): 604–25.
37. The best summary of the phenomenon, and the main source for the account offered here, is the chapter "La 'statuomanie' et l'histoire," in Maurice Agulhon, *Histoire vagabonde*, vol. 1, *Ethnologie et politique dans la France contemporaine* (Paris: Gallimard, 1988), 137–85.

of civic and national identity and the locus of key partisan political struggles: both the Left and the Right recognized the stakes involved in celebrating their heroes in statues. Thus, it is not surprising that Louis XVIII promulgated an ordinance in 1816 specifying, "In the future, no gift, no homage, no recompense can be voted, offered or discerned as a testimony of public recognition, by departmental councils, city councils, national guards, or any other civil or military body, without our prior authorization."[38] The decree led to the establishment of a small bureaucracy to deal with proposals for monuments and to the most systematic form of censorship in nineteenth-century France pertaining to the plastic arts. Henceforth, the patron, who could vary from a single person to a large committee, a municipality, or the national government, had to gain approval from this office. Only then could the organizers proceed to the many other activities that these projects entailed: the purchase or commission of a sculpture, or the staging of a *concours*; the organization, if necessary, of a subscription; and the inaugural ceremonies.

We know surprisingly little about the operation and decisions of this bureaucracy, though in-depth studies are now underway.[39] Clear cases of politically motivated censorship were apparently rare, but the office facilitated and impeded requests. Projects were primarily scuttled by having any decision on them deferred indefinitely. Agulhon notes that one application for a monument to the doctor François-Xavier Bichat in Bourg-en-Bresse, put forth by the Société d'émulation de l'Ain, was apparently too much in the spirit of the Enlightenment for the Restoration, and the dossier was allowed to gather dust permanently.[40] We will of course never know how many monuments were never proposed because they were politically unviable, nor how many and what type of monuments might have been erected had censorship not existed.

38. Ordonnance no. 898, 10 July 1816, *Bulletin des lois*. 1816 (2nd semester), 43–44. Such homages included the naming of streets, concessions in communal cemeteries, and the occasional individual honor, such as the awarding of a sword, or a commemorative bust.

39. Catherine Chevillot, "Orner ou ne pas orner, la série des hommages publics aux Archives nationales," lecture at the Archives nationales, Paris, 20 October 2009. Chevillot is in the process of examining the archival records of the office charged with reviewing all requests for "public homages," kept in the Archives Nationales, cote F1c I, dossiers 137–186, 189–197 ter. Her research has thus far focused on the Second Empire. I thank her for making her findings available to me.

40. Agulhon, *Histoire vagabonde*, 163.

Among those that were approved, clear trends may be observed. In contrast to the Empire's penchant for commemorating military men, the Restoration privileged royalty and its loyal servants, but in the provinces a taste for commemorating exceptional men of culture emerged even in the face of the government's priority of restoring statues of kings. The July Monarchy saw a marked increase in public statuary and adhered to the meritocratic aspect of statuomania: the regime witnessed a profusion of monuments devoted to Revolutionary and Imperial soldiers, men of letters, science, and the arts, and local benefactors and philanthropists. The Second Republic had little time to establish its own policies, but by and large continued the same trends as the preceding regime.[41]

Perhaps the most dramatic censorship of public monuments took place not behind the doors of government offices but out in the streets with hammers and axes. Vandalism was the chief means by which public sculptures were removed from view, and it was often sanctioned, ordered, or carried out by the government. Oddly, it has rarely been considered in discussions of censorship despite the fact that its main purpose was to suppress images with politically objectionable content.[42]

Vandalism was an integral part of Revolutionary culture. Revolutionaries destroyed or defaced many key royal, aristocratic, and religious monuments, and often built their own monuments where the old ones had stood, a practice continued by Napoleon. The Revolution destroyed the major equestrian portraits of Bourbon kings that decorated squares and roundabouts in Paris, and the Restoration spent an equal amount of time tearing down whatever the Revolution had put in their place and restoring, as far as was possible, the earlier statuary. Thus, on the Pont Neuf, François-Frédéric Lemot created a new statue of Henri XIV, using the bronze from three Napoleonic sculptures: the reliefs from a monument in Boulogne, the statue of Louis Desaix from the place des Victoires, and the statue of Napoleon from

41. Agulhon, *Histoire vagabonde*, 158–64. The most complete catalog of the statues is France Debuisson et al., *À nos grands hommes, la sculpture publique de la Révolution à la seconde guerre mondiale*, CD-ROM, ed. Catherine Chevillot and Chantal Georgel (Paris: Musée d'Orsay/INHA/France Debuisson/Laurent Chastel, 2004). The number of monuments approved under the regimes in question here (with the Napoleonic regime included for reference) is as follows: 1799–1814: 28; 1814–1830: 61; 1830–1848: 159; 1848–1852: 77.

42. For a synthetic account of vandalism, see Louis Réau, *Les monuments détruits de l'art français*, 2 vols. (Paris: Hachette, 1959).

atop the column in the place Vendôme. Charles Dupaty sculpted a new Louis XIII for the place Royale (place des Vosges), which had remained empty since the Revolution. François-Joseph Bosio produced a Louis XIV for the place des Victoires, where Desaix had once stood. A new Louis XV was commissioned from Pierre Cartellier for the place de la Concorde, but delays and the decision to commemorate Louis XVI in the spot displaced this monument to the roundabout at the bottom of the Champs-Elysées, and it was not completed before the fall of the Restoration.[43]

Existing monuments were redecorated with changes in regime. In Paris, in particular, the changes were substantial. Such major landmarks as the Pantheon and the Arc du Carrousel had their sculptural decorations repeatedly and significantly altered over the course of the first half of the nineteenth century, and others, such as the Arc de Triomphe de l'Étoile, were completed in forms radically different from those initially envisioned.[44] The best known example is the Vendôme column, built on the site of François Girardon's statue of Louis XIV, which had been destroyed in 1792 on orders of the Revolutionary government. In 1800 the Consulate projected a column commemorating the fallen soldiers of the department of the Seine for the site, and shortly thereafter Napoleon considered placing a statue of Charlemagne taken from Aix-la-Chapelle atop the column. After the victory in Austerlitz in 1805, the plan changed again: Vivant Denon, Napoleon's Director of the Arts, taking his cue from the Column of Trajan, commissioned a long relief spiraling up the column of the Austrian campaign from Pierre-Nolasque Bergeret, and a statue of Napoleon as an emperor in Roman dress to stand at the top from Antoine-Denis Chaudet. The Restoration replaced Napoleon with a white flag decorated with a fleur-de-lis, while the July Monarchy returned the column somewhat to its original aspect by commissioning a statue from Emile Seurre of Napoleon in his military uniform (and,

43. For synthetic accounts, see June Hargrove, *The Statues of Paris: An Open Air Pantheon* (New York: The Vendome Press, 1989), 53–58; Réunion des musées nationaux, *La sculpture française au XIXe siècle* (Paris: Réunion des musées nationaux, 1986); and Père de Bertier, "Nouvelles statues royales," in *Art ou politique? Arcs, statues et colonnes de Paris*, ed. Geneviève Bresc-Bautier and Xavier Dectot (Paris: Action artistique de la ville de Paris, 1999), 106–109.

44. Isabelle Rouge, "L'Arc de Triomphe de l'Étoile," in Bresc-Bautier and Dectot, 99–105, 122–126; Neil McWilliam, "David d'Angers and the Panthéon Commission: Politics and Public Works under the July Monarchy," *Art History* 5/2 (December, 1982): 426–46.

pointedly, not as a Roman emperor). Napoleon III replaced Seurre's statue with a replica of Chaudet's original sculpture. In 1871 the Communards, led by Gustave Courbet in his capacity as President of the Commission of Fine Arts of the provisional government, toppled the column, and the Versailles government almost immediately ordered its restoration, which was completed under the Third Republic.[45]

This history of vandalism and redesign contains within it a shift of great significance for our subject. While the Revolution and the Restoration treated the public decorations of the preceding regimes as objects to be censored, the July Monarchy began to look upon them as cultural heritage. Of course the July Monarchy had its own record of vandalism. For example, a relief on the Palais Bourbon of Law flanked by Might and Justice, executed by Alexandre-Evariste Fragonard in 1816, was broken up and replaced by France flanked by Liberty and Order, executed by Jean-Pierre Cortot in 1839.[46] Moreover, the July Monarchy's policy toward monuments of past regimes was far from disinterested: it belonged to a broader effort by Louis-Philippe to create an inclusive historical account of France that represented his own government as the logical solution to a politically divisive recent past. The citizen-king was particularly interested in co-opting the Revolutionary and Napoleonic legacies and diffusing their threat to his regime by magnanimously celebrating their acceptable achievements. However self-serving the July Monarchy's policy may have been, it nonetheless balanced questions of artistic achievement and historic preservation with those of political significance and censorship. This pointed to the future, when the destruction of the Vendôme column during the Commune was condemned by the Third Republic not as a political act, but as an atavistic act of iconoclasm that destroyed a work of art and a piece of the national heritage. Public statuary was becoming less important as an overt expression of partisan political power, even if different regimes favored different types of figures and themes. In relation to the growth of statuary commemorating great

45. See Georges Poisson, "L'Empereur, colonne Vendôme," in Bresc-Bautier and Dectot, 94; and "La colonne Vendôme," in Bresc-Bautier and Dectot, 156–57. A very suggestive overview of the column's history is in Albert Boime, *Hollow Icons: The Politics of Sculpture in Nineteenth-Century France* (Kent, Ohio: Kent State University Press, 1987), 6–13.

46. Agulhon, *Marianne into Battle: Republican Imagery and Symbolism in France, 1789–1880* (Cambridge: Cambridge University Press, 1981), 43.

men in the second half of the century, Agulhon comments, "Erecting a statue would henceforth no longer mean celebrating the conqueror on the debris of the statue of the conquered; now it meant to enshrine a celebrity, almost beside the older statues."[47]

Over the course of the period from 1815 to 1852, certain patterns emerged. Politics and battles around censorship increasingly focused on the masses and thus on printed media. Censorship certainly existed for items such as paintings and sculpture, clocks and clothing, or flags and liberty trees, but these objects received varying treatment. Objects created for the consumption by the lower classes generally elicited greater concern than those directed at the well-to-do. The police worried more about flags, pipes, and kerchiefs than about clocks, jewelry, and silverware, just as they worried more about popular prints as opposed to artistic ones. Painting was scarcely touched. It was to some extent already controlled through its reliance on government patronage or on the confining strictures of the exhibition and the art market. Art itself was increasingly devoted to private and individualistic forms of expression, and often expressed itself in learned, experimental, or avant-garde modes. But for the most part the government generally allowed it to explore any subject in relative freedom. Sculpture is a hybrid case: to the extent that it was public, political, and viewed by the masses it received attention, but increasingly it was not the site of partisan political battles, and as art or as cultural heritage it was increasingly ignored by censors.

If art did not engage the censors' fears in part because of its elite nature, we might say that political emblems were, in contrast, not sufficiently sophisticated to merit the same attention as political caricature. To begin with, such objects were easily fashioned by almost anyone, rendering censorship somewhat futile. But perhaps more importantly, they were not particularly nuanced in their political message. In Peircian terms, their significance was primarily indexical: they relied on their association with the events, groups, and regimes with which they had co-occurred, but they lacked the sophisticated iconic and symbolic means that other media possessed. In other words, their meanings carried profound emotional resonance because of their close association with key ideas and events, but they could not express complex interpretations and narratives as well as a

47. Agulhon, *Histoire vagabonde*, 303–304.

text or discursive image. In sum, they were important expressions of political affiliation but did not articulate political ideas with nuance to large numbers of people.

In our own day objects are sometimes excepted from censorship on the basis of artistic merit, yet in the period in question here art was excepted from censorship primarily because the government was much more interested in a nascent mass culture, which was rarely considered artistic. Today, as they did in the first half of the nineteenth century, people perceive and treat different categories of visual culture differently, but for the nineteenth-century mind one might go so far as to say that the idea of visual culture would not have made much sense. Things visual concerned the government because in general they seemed more accessible to the masses, but what mattered still more was the place and purpose of the object in society: whether an object was part of elite or subordinate culture, whether or not it was capable of influencing the masses, whether it posed a threat or not to the dominant social and political orders.[48]

48. I wish to thank Robert Goldstein, Sheryl Kroen, Catherine Chevillot, Ségolène Le Men, and Claire Babillon for their generous help in the preparation of this article.

JUDITH WECHSLER

Daumier and Censorship, 1866–1872

After fourteen years of drawing Parisian customs, manners, and hab-
its, in 1866, Honoré Daumier recommenced producing political caricatures. What caused this shift? From 1835–1848 and starting again
with the reign of Napoleon III in 1852, censorship laws prohibited
caricatures of political subjects. Though there was not an explicit
change in the laws in the period from 1866 to 1872, enforcement became more variable and lenient. Daumier and the editors of *Le charivari* ventured back into the political arena, cautiously. From 1866
when the application of censorship began to loosen, until 1872, the
majority of Daumier's 463 caricatures had political references.

   In this article, I will review the censorship laws and the changes in
their implementation, and focus on some of Daumier's political caricatures, a few of which concern the press explicitly. I will juxtapose
the government's changes in attitude toward censorship from year to
year and some of the subjects Daumier addressed.

   While we do not know the exact criteria for the censors' judgment,
we can, in part, deduce them from Daumier's political caricature—
what he represented and by what visual means. But we must also
consider how the preclusions of censorship might have made possible
certain kinds of artistic achievement.

   There was no invention with what Baudelaire called the "ar-
got plastique," or plastic slang, comparable to the pear, invented
by Daumier and his editor Philipon, as the symbol for King Louis-
Philippe from 1831–1835. But Daumier does introduce new figures,
particularly that of the jester, holding a large pen, who bears witness,
emblematic of his own activity as a caricaturist. I will further consider some of the inventions of this period, and the opportunities

YFS 122, *Out of Sight: Political Censorship of the Visual Arts in Nineteenth-Century France,* ed. Goldstein, © 2012 by Yale University.

wrung from the obstacle of censorship: by indirection Daumier found new directions.

Censorship was enforced after the demise of the Second Republic and the reestablishment of the monarchy under Napoleon III, prohibiting publication of political caricatures. The act of February 17, 1852, Article 22, which quoted verbatim from the September Laws of 1835, prevailed throughout much of the Second Empire.

> No drawings, engravings, lithographs, medallions, prints, or emblems of any kind may be published, displayed, or sold without the prior authorization of the Ministry of the Police of Paris or the prefects of the departments.
>
> In the event of violation, the drawings, prints, engravings, lithographs, medallions, and emblems will be confiscated by the courts of correction [i.e. magistrate sitting without a jury] and those who published them sentenced to a prison term of one month to a year, and a fine of 100 to 1000 Francs without precluding prosecution resulting from publication, exhibition or sale of the aforesaid objects.[1]

Authority for the censorship laws shifted in 1858 from the Bureau of Printing and Bookstores in the Police Division to the Public Security Administration which, under the Vicomte de la Guéronnière, was renamed the *Division de l'imprimerie, de la librairie et de la propriété littéraire* (Bureau of the press, bookstores, and literary property.)[2] The laws were implemented by the prefects, who were regarded as "in-

---

1. Gustave Rousset, *Code général des lois sur la presse et autre moyen de publication.* (Paris, 1869), 223. Translations are my own throughout this article. See also Armand Ravelet, *Code manuel de la presse: comprenant toutes les lois sur l'imprimerie, la librairie, la presse périodique . . .* [Ressource électronique] 2002; Robert Justin Goldstein, *Censorship of Political Caricature in Nineteenth Century France* (Kent, Ohio, 1989), 11, for explanatory notes in parentheses; Patrick Laharie, *Contrôle de la presse, de la librairie et du colportage sous le Second Empire, 1852–1879,* XII, Inventaires des articles F18 266 à 293 (Paris, Archives nationales, 1995). F¹⁸ 265 à 293, 552–555, 566–571, 2345. Laharie includes descriptions of the contents of the file numbers for the laws regarding the press; Archives nationales inventory, *Contrôle de la presse sous le second empire,* XII; Claude Bélanger, Jacques Godechot, Pierre Guiral, and Fernand Terrou, eds., *Histoire générale de la presse française.* (Paris, 1969), vol. II, 1815–1871; *Bulletin des lois de la République française.* Michelle Thery, who worked for 30 years at the Assemblée nationale, tracked down some of the information in various files and books at the Archives nationales, the Bibliothèque nationale de France, and at the Assemblée nationale. I am very grateful to her. My thanks also to Christopher Ricks for editorial corrections and suggestions.

2. Brondel, e-mail of 11 August 2010. Nicole Brondel, a nineteenth-century specialist at the Archives nationales, was most helpful identifying and communicating information in relevant files and documents.

struments of this repression." In 1860, the duc de Persigny, an ardent follower of Napoleon III, became Minister of the Interior for a second time until 1863 and was responsible for overseeing censorship once again through the Public Security Administration, which was under the direct surveillance of his office. Political newspapers had to deposit a large sum in advance as caution money. The secret police were actively employed in surveillance, intimidation, and repression.[3] Warnings, suspensions, and suppressions were persistent threats.[4]

As the government did not articulate the changing criteria for the application of the censorship laws in these years, the censors were given greater flexibility in deciding whether to condemn images they deemed offensive or threatening. Lucien Prévost-Paradol, a satirical writer, declared in 1868 that "the law has much less importance in press matters than the jurisdiction, since the law cannot avoid being vague and leave a large place to the whim of the judge."[5] In the albums at the Archives nationales that record the images submitted to the censors for the years 1866–1872,[6] in the column marked "observations," the notes often indicate only the kind of object deposited and whether the work was accepted or rejected, sometimes specifying who made the decision (e.g., the prefect of the police or a minister). Most often these notes concerned the images that were censored, marked "refusé."[7]

The *Code générale des lois sur la presse et autre moyen de publication* details the infractions and penalties.[8] Information concerning what the censors specifically might have found offensive was not given: at times they refused to sign even official statements of approval or rejection. Nicole Brondel recounts that the editor or the illustrator could approach the censor for an explanation, and reasons would be given orally. But it was not possible to appeal the decision.

As the censored works were not published, though some survived, it is difficult to establish the specific criteria for their rejection, which were not made public. There were, however, various guidelines that

3. Brondel, e-mail of 11 August 2010

4. Henry Zeldin. *France 1848–1945*, Volume II: *Intellect, Taste and Anxiety* (Oxford, 1977), 547.

5. Goldstein, 24

6. Archives nationales, Paris, F18* 7 to 13, *Enregistrement de déclaration de matériel d'imprimerie et de presse, 1853–1881*, F 18* 27–31, *Enregistrement des estampes, gravures et dessins*, 1863–1881, F/18(I)/26 à 31.

7. F/18(I)/28 to 31.

8. See note 1.

highlighted the causes for censorship:[9] anything that could undermine the authority of the Chief of State and of foreign sovereign leaders; anything that undermined religion (including morals); defamation of or insult to the tribunals; anything that could be seen as subverting the social order (like a picture of poverty in France).[10]

The exact procedures changed considerably from year to year, reflecting not only the changing political climate but also frequent changes of interior ministers and heads of the relevant divisions and bureaus within the ministry. Between 1865 and 1869, there were three different Ministers of the Interior.[11]

Louis Napoleon's government, from about 1866, not only wanted to appear more liberal, but also to encourage all forms of commerce, including publications of journals and books. Censorship of theaters was also diminished at this time, largely for commercial reasons.[12] The attitude of the government toward censorship became more one of "closing one's eyes."

For each of the years from 1866 to 1872 I will highlight some particularly indicative, characteristic, or significant works, with emphasis on those images with explicit reference to the press or censorship. I urge the reader to study the Daumier catalog to get a sense of his overall production during these years.[13] All but one of the Daumier lithographs referred to were published in *Le charivari*, the principal liberal newspaper that featured a large caricature daily.[14]

Of the approximately 77 Daumier caricatures published in *Le charivari* in 1866, 33 caricatures concern Europe, and 17 specifically about France. Several refer to the press and censorship. The caricature "Taking the articles of Mr. de Girardin too seriously and offering their services" (23 January, D. 3480) refers to the ambitious liberal publisher whom Napoleon III particularly disliked. A funeral cortege, with two men dressed in black and a dark carriage driven by a man with a Napoleonic hat, is at the door marked "to the Press" with a poster advertising Émile de Girardin's "Letter to A Dead Man." In

9. Such as *Documents pour servir à l'histoire du second empire. Circulaires, rapports, notes et instructions confidentielles. 1851–1870 /1872* : http://gallica.bnf.fr/ark:/12148/bpt6k5426650b

10. Brondel, e-mail of 11 August 2010.

11. Goldstein, 14.

12. Conversation with Brondel, June 14, 2010.

13. All Daumier's lithographs can be viewed at www.daumier- register.org

14. The works are identified by Delteil catalog numbers, indicated as D. Lois Delteil, *Le Peintre-Graveur Illustré, Daumier* (New York, NY, 1969).

"A quarter hour after his death, he's still alive" (20 February, D. 3486), a rare double page cartoon with words incorporated, refers again to the text above and to other of Girardin's writings. He is shown being carried out on a stretcher by three women in mourning, including his wife and sister. An old woman carries a sign, "The Press, an Idea each day." Three cripples represent young and healthy ideas. From under the skirts of the press, ducks (rumors) fly out bearing signs marked "Bulletin," "stock market," "confidence," and "impotence."[15] The words that appear in the lithograph make specific reference to what might otherwise be interpreted more broadly.

"And these two old wrecks console each other" (15 May, D. 3500) shows Girardin embracing politician Émile Ollivier. Although a Republican sent into exile in 1851 for his opposition to Louis Napoleon, Ollivier returned in 1860, accepted the Empire, and served as a cabinet minister in the hope of winning some concessions toward a constitutional monarchy. In 1866–67 he formed a political party that supported the principle of a liberal Empire, which included relaxation of the press laws. Daumier draws him repeatedly. The newspaper, *La liberté*, shown on a poster in the background, published by Girardin, became the unofficial voice for Ollivier's party. Caricaturing individuals was generally prohibited, unless they gave their permission. Can we assume then that Girardin and Ollivier agreed to be caricatured? Here we don't see their faces, so it may not have been necessary to have their approval, but they also might not have objected. Evidence of the move toward a more liberal Empire can be seen in the revival of the series of *"Actualités"* (Current Events) in *Le charivari*, in response to pressure from the public who wanted to know more about the foreign exploits and the wars. Many of Daumier's political caricatures would appear in this series.

In the last years of the Second Empire, international conflict took center stage. Napoleon III had made France into a major military power, entering into wars with almost every important country in Europe except England. The military engagement of France with Italy, Russia, Austria, Prussia, and Turkey unsettled the European balance of power. Daumier focuses on the perils of France in the international scheme. The motif of instability would recur repeatedly in the coming years. In "European Equilibrium" (1 December, D. 3540) the globe is balanced on the bayonets of many countries, referring to

15. Daumier register.

the perilous European situation growing out of the Prussian victory over Austria. "New Aerial Suspension" (7 February, 1867, D. 3552) depicts Europe as an allegorical female figure balanced on a bayonet, and the same year, Europe is shown balanced on a lit bomb (3 April 1867, D. 3566, Fig. 1). The figure of Europe, shown as substantial

Figure 1. Honoré Daumier, "European Equilibrium." *Le charivari*, April 3, 1867. (D. 3566) Benjamin A. and Julia M. Trustman Collection of Honoré Daumier Lithographs. Robert D. Farber University Archives and Special Collections Department, Brandeis University.

and dynamic, suggested by the charged lines, just keeps her balance. This monumental figure and the other allegorical ones Daumier uses at this time, recall his powerful figures such as *La République* and washerwomen carrying their burden. He incorporates qualities seen in his paintings, watercolors, and drawings, as one of the inventive means of countering the constraints of censorship.

While it was generally presumed that images were more dangerous and undermining than words, it was often the caption that triggered the censor's refusal. In a private collection in Germany, there are some 13 Daumier lithographs submitted to the censors with their marks in the margin, indicating *oui* or *non*, yes or no. For example, in 1866, Ollivier is shown from the back (D. 3484), trying to decide which way to turn, "right or left." The caricature was censored because of the caption and resubmitted with an altered legend— *"bien embarrassé"* (pretty embarrassed), also rejected. This image was never published. Daumier did not write his captions; rather they were provided by one of the editors at *Le charivari*. So it is ironic that the censor would dismiss his drawing on the basis of the text. Daumier is reputed to have said that he did not think captions were necessary. Perhaps he did not want the potential multivalence of his image to be pinned down.

While caricaturists and their publishers increasingly dared to defy or subvert the restrictions of censorship, certain subjects were clearly out of bounds: representations of Napoleon III remained forbidden. André Gill drew one cartoon of the Emperor in 1867 for *La lune*, which was censored and there are no further examples. There are relatively few *portraits-charges* in the period 1852–1881, as they required consent. Goldstein notes, however, that this law was not enforced between 1869 and 1874.[16]

With declining popularity due in part to economic grievances, and with the rising power of Prussia and the collapse of French Imperial adventures in Mexico in 1867, Napoleon III promised reforms in an attempt to placate his liberal opponents. In a letter dated January 19, 1867, addressed to Ernest Rouher, the authoritarian Minister of State, the Emperor wrote that a new law would be announced shortly regarding the press and promised concessions, including an end to the

16. Goldstein, 16. I have not been able to find other documents to confirm this observation.

administrative law established in 1852.[17] There were long delays before the bill was brought to the *Corps législatif*, and debate did not begin until January 19, 1868, more than a year after the Emperor's promise. Dropping the requirement for preliminary authorization when a journal was founded was significant. Government officials were no longer allowed to warn, suspend, or suppress journals. But certain concessions to freedom of the press were still withheld: trial by jury was refused, and correctional tribunals were maintained. The new law still left the authorities with considerable power if they wanted to exert it. Collins cites two handbooks that listed 269 legal provisions that journalists needed to follow to be safe from the tribunals.[18]

The strict implementation of censorship of caricatures concerning internal politics is probably the reason that only 17 of Daumier's 70 published caricatures in 1867 make reference to France, and at that, rather broadly. Forty caricatures concern European affairs, with a focus on Prussia, the danger of armaments, and the threat to peace. *Halte!!!* (4 June, D. 3575) shows a Frenchman trying to keep the trains, marked Prussia and France, from colliding. A few months later, the jester is drawn looking out over a field of tombstones, with the caption. "To think that with the stones of all these pedestals one would have been able to build a good dozen primary schools" (19 October, D. 3600). The motif appears again with the caption, "Forced to draw a new map of an area now used for military exercises, which used to be the location of the 'Temple of Peace'" (26 November, D. 3610).

Among the extant lithographs of 1867 with the different captions presented to the censors is "Madame is moving!" (1867, D. 3590), showing a skeleton with a scythe, the figure of death, riding on top of a locomotive. This refers critically to the government's policy to build railroads, for military reasons, to the eastern borders of France— in the direction of Germany.[19] Daumier anticipates the terrible consequences. The original caption, "The cemeteries are being moved. Hooray! The dead are coming fast" was submitted by Destouches, the printer, on September 2, as marked on one of the proofs, rejected on September 9, 1867, and replaced by the caption, "Voyagers to Eternity," which was also refused. The caption was then crossed out by

17. Irene Collins, *The Government and the Newspaper Press in France 1814–1881* (London: Oxford University Press, 1959), 147.

18. Collins, 148, referring to Ravelet and Rousset, see footnote 1.

19. Daumier register.

the publisher's hand and replaced with the third version of the caption, "Madame (sc la Mort) déménage." The caricature was not published. Images that were approved were marked with a large stamp, diminishing their value for collectors.[20]

New liberal press laws went into effect on May 11, 1868, after a vote of the Assemblée nationale to replace the requirement for prior authorization *(supprimer l'autorisation préalable)* as cited in articles 1 and 32 of the decree of February 17, 1852. The cautionary tax *(cautionnement)* was dropped, as well as the stamp tax *(le droit de timbre)*, for some journals and reduced for others, allowing for the creation of less expensive journals. However, a deposit of 50,000 francs was required, replacing the listing of violations. The correctional tribunals were abandoned in favor of juries.[21]

At the same time, the regime, when it felt threatened or offended, remained repressive. Though there were ongoing collisions with the press, Guiral states that after 1868, it knew a freedom almost as great as that at the start of the Second Republic.[22]

The Law Relative to the Press of 11 May 1868 states:[23]

Article 1. Every Frenchman with civil and political rights can publish a journal or periodical that appears regularly and on a fixed date, and whether by delivery or irregularly, without a preliminary authorization.

Article 2. No journal or written periodical can be published if it is not presented, in Paris, to the prefecture of the police, and in the departments, to the prefecture, at least 15 days before publication, with a declaration that contains the following:

1. The title of the journal or periodical and when it will appear.
2. The name, address and rights of the owners other than the sleeping partners *(commanditaires)*.
3. The name and address of the editor.
4. The press where it will be printed.

Any change to the enumerated conditions above must be declared in the 15 days that follow.

20. Hans-Juergen Hellwig, "Honoré Daumier—a Fighter for the Republic," in Habersack, Hommelhoff, Hueffner, and Schmidt, eds., *Commemorative Publication on the Occasion of the 70th Birthday of Peter Ulmer* (De Gruyter Recht: Berlin, 2003), 7.

21. E-mail from Brondel, 17 June 2010.

22. Guiral, 45.

23. Laharie, xii.

Any infraction of the provisions of the present article is punished as mentioned in article 5 of the decree of 17 February 1852.

. . . .

Article 16. Articles 1 and 32 of the decree of 17 February 1852 are repealed and generally the dispositions of the previous laws, which are contrary to the present law.

The suspension, in the case presumed by article 9 of the decree of 17 February 1852, can only be declared by the judiciary authority.

The details regarding the ways the law was to be implemented indicate its repressive effect.[24] There are only nine political caricatures of France among the 71 Daumier published in *Le charivari* in 1868. Forty-four concern Europe with a focus on arms and the danger to peace. "The statues of the future" (29 April, D. 3637) features the inventors of armaments. "Après Vous!!! . . ." (4 May, D. 3640) shows a Prussian officer gesturing toward a door marked "Bureau of Disarmament," while his French counterpart turns away with the classic pose of demurring. The threat to peace recurs in "Renewing the Turenne," where the allegorical figure of Peace is pictured asleep on a cannon (15 June, D. 3644), and "Attention!" (1 July 1868, D. 3548), where Peace flies into cobwebs marked "Question of Romaine, Orient, Germany . . ."

There are caricatures critical of the plebiscite, the elections, and the impact they had in leading the country to war. The predominant themes in 1868 are the Prussians and the threat of war, specifically Prussia's victory over Austria, the figure of Mars-god of war, the Greek uprising against Turkey in Crete, and inflation.

"The blank newspaper" (31 March, D. 3631, Fig. 2) makes direct reference to censorship in favor of the free press. The government had tried to pass a bill that would prohibit the press from reporting in the daily newspapers on the lives of individuals. The jester, pen and feather dangling from his belt, holds up a blank page, marked "*La Vie Privée*" (private life), suggesting that it is better to leave the pages blank since the papers would no longer be able to criticize publicly politicians and corrupt administrators.[25] The proposed article 11 of the law of 11 May 1868 read: "Every publication in a periodical rela-

24. Rousset, *Code général des lois sur la presse et autre moyen de publication;* 222.
25. Daumier register.

ACTUALITÉS   72.

LA VIE PRIVÉE

LE JOURNAL EN BLANC.

Figure 2. Honoré Daumier, "The Blank Newspaper." *Le charivari*, March 31, 1868. (D. 3631) By permission of the Daumier Register. www.daumier-register.org

tive to a fact of a person's personal life constitutes a contravention punished by a fine of 500 francs. This can be applied only upon complaint by the interested party."[26]

In "The Spring Tide of 1868" (19 December, D. 3681), politician Adolphe Thiers is attacked by newspapers from all sides, depicted as overhead flying ducks (*canards*), symbol of newspaper hoaxes. Thiers,

26. *Extrait de la circulaire du ministère de la police générale aux préfets.* Archives nationale, 10a.

who had been prime minister under Louis-Philippe, voted for Louis Napoleon and reentered political life as a representative in 1863 as a liberal monarchist. This caricature refers to the new liberal press laws of March 9, 1868, which led to many entrepreneurs investing in newspapers, most of which did not last. The *canards* rapidly grew in production and were put out of business by the government to stop the flood of misinformation.[27]

In April 1869 a constitutional monarchy was proclaimed. That year there were many more caricatures concerning France, suggesting greater liberty for political satire. Of the 70 Daumier lithographs published, 60 concern France with emphasis on the parliamentary election of May 1869 and its destructive role. There are seven caricatures concerning Europe. Three caricatures are non-political.

Elections are a prevalent theme. When Émile Ollivier shifted from the opposition to follow Napoleon III as a liberal monarchist, *Le charivari* waged a campaign to defeat him, through editorials and numerous caricatures by Daumier. He sought a ministry not recognized by the constitution. There is a *portrait-charge* of Ollivier, with a huge nose and bat wings, standing in front of an electoral urn, smiling broadly. The caption, quoting La Fontaine, reads "I am a bird, see my wings, I am a bat, long live the rats" (24 March, D. 3700). Ollivier is also depicted in the Chamber of Deputies, in "Between Two Saddles" (15 April, D. 3705, Fig. 3), where he is pictured having been toppled while performing a balancing act between two horses who race around the Assembly floor as in a circus or hippodrome.

"The day after the battle" depicts the day after the election (25 May, D. 3713) when the Emperor's party lost more than a million votes. Daumier draws a field of felled figures, the one in front, pictured with an electoral urn on his stomach. A few months later Daumier draws an unruly parliament where no one listens to the speaker, suggesting the ineffectiveness of the Chamber (8 July, D. 3721).

Napoleon III accepted a compromise in July 1869 orchestrated by Ollivier, further loosening censorship restrictions. The Republicans won thirty seats, the monarchists forty-six. But the center Right party had the largest victory, gaining 126 seats and coming under the leadership of Ollivier. With *V'là ma cartouche* (This is my bullet) (20 November, D.3746), a man points to the ballot in his hand. In the background the crowd is looking at a wall with posters marked "Can-

27. Daumier register.

ACTUALITÉS   63.

Enlre deux selles

Figure 3. Honoré Daumier, "Between Two Saddles." April 15, 1869. (D. 3705)
Benjamin A. and Julia M. Trustmon Collection of Honoré Daumier Lithographs. Robert D. Farber University Archives and Special Collection Department, Brandeis University.

didate" and a doorway marked "Election." Daumier is urging citizens
to vote: the ballot is like a bullet—a weapon.[28]

One of the most significant developments in Daumier's political
caricatures in this period is the frequent deployment of female allegorical figures. In addition to the figure of Europe, Daumier draws
Liberty, Diplomacy, and France. Sometimes the figures of France and
Liberty are interchangeable. There are male allegorical figures representing Austria, Germany, England, Ireland, Spain, and Jamaica and a

28. Daumier register.

Figure 4. Honoré Daumier, "She definitely has a stronger voice." *Le chari-vari*, June 23, 1869. (D. 3717) Benjamin A. and Julia M. Trustman Collection of Honoré Daumier Lithographs. Robert D. Farber University Archives and Special Collections Department, Brandeis University.

female representing Venice. After 1870, Daumier revives the figure of the Republic whose image had been popular in 1848–1850.[29] He draws Liberty seven times in 1869. With *Elle a décidément plus de voix* ("She definitely has a stronger voice") (23 June, D. 3717, Fig. 4), the figure of the jester looks on as Liberty sings, accompanying herself on

---

29. See Hollis Clayson, *Paris in Despair: Art and Everyday Life under Siege, 1870–71* (Chicago: University of Chicago Press, 2002).

the piano. Daumier combines the allegorical and the emblematic: the personification of an ideal witnessed by the caricaturist. She is not caricatured: certain kinds of beauty are inimical to an art whose language employs exaggeration. As Angus Fletcher observes, even when allegory appears naturalistic in caricature, exaggerating real traits, it nevertheless turns the real into an abstraction. "Allegories are the natural mirrors of ideology."[30] Allegory was one of the principal ways in which Daumier could convey his political criticism and be less vulnerable to censorship using personifications rather than caricaturing a person. His allegorical figures go beyond the moment and the particular to embody and communicate a larger concept. Idealized and principled, the allegorical figures could not be censored, as were more specific references to politicians and events. Though not referring to Daumier, what Fletcher notes is apt: "This subversive style, sometimes satirical, sometimes utopian . . . preserves freedom against tyranny. Allegory presumably thrives on political censorship."[31]

By using allegorical figures in contemporary circumstances, Daumier refers to both the quotidian and the "eternal," qualities, which for Baudelaire, are required for great art. "Excuse me my dear, let us verify my powers before yours!" (16 July, D. 3724) shows the noble and calm figure of Liberty, arm upraised in a sign of rejection, holding back Mars, god of war, shown as an old warrior in classic garb and plumed helmet, who recoils in the traditional gesture of surprise. In the background are a cannon and cannon balls. This image probably refers to parliamentary sessions between June 28 and July 12 when the distribution of powers was being regulated. Fletcher notes that "allegory appears to express conflict between moral authorities. The mode is hierarchical in essence . . . it tells them what their legitimate powers are."[32] In another optimistic image, Liberty is shown lighting fireworks with the words "social and political progress": "The true firework is to be liberal" (14 August, D. 3728). The female figure of France projects a sign "Liberty" from her magic lantern (19 November, D. 3745).[33] Ségolène Le Men points out that the word "Liberty" appears in a number of lithographs from this period, referring both to

30. Angus Fletcher, *Allegory, the Theory of a Symbolic Mode* (Ithaca: Cornell University Press, 1974), 368.

31. Fletcher, 328.

32. Fletcher, 22.

33. Ségolène Le Men, "Une lithographie de Daumier en 1869: Lanterne magique!," *Revue d'histoire du XIXe siècle* (2000) : 13–37.

Figure 5. Honoré Daumier, "I think the umbrella will wind up broken." *Le charivari*, 23 October 1869 (D. 3743) By permission of the Daumier Register. www.daumier-register.org

the presumed greater liberty of the Empire and the new freedom of expression.[34]

Words appear in a number of Daumier's caricatures as keys to interpretation, whether to contemporary issues such as "La vie privée," "Bloc electoral," "Libre pensée," or an entity or institution, such as the "Constitution," "France," or "République." In "I think the

34. Le Men, *Daumier et la caricature* (Paris : Citadelles & Mazenod, 2008), 211.

umbrella will wind up broken" (23 October, D. 3743, Fig. 5), two frightened anxious men are huddled under an umbrella marked "Article 75" that shields them from the newspapers mounted on wooden posts that are raining down on them. This was during the time of the campaign concerning revocation of the censorship laws, proposed by the opposition in the new article 75, to dissolve the old system as of September 10, 1870, which would have dismantled the administrative structures that involved many employees.[35] The two men depicted are probably representative of the employees threatened by the changes.

Despite *Le charivari*'s critical stance toward Ollivier, who became Minister of Justice in 1870, he continued to support a liberal program of press legislation, which may suggest that he gave permission to be caricatured, or, as Goldstein notes, perhaps the rule was not assiduously applied. Ollivier introduced a bill to the *Corps législatif* on January 26, 1870, referring press cases to trial by jury.[36] Two days later, Ollivier wrote to the Procureur Général of the Cabinet du Garde des Sceaux, which gives clear evidence of the increased discretion of judgment allowed to the censors:[37]

Paris, 28 January 1870

Minister of Justice and Religion
Office of the Guard of Sceaux

Circular

Monsieur le Procureur Général,

A complete regulation of the press implies three different orders of resolutions: those regarding repression, those regarding competence, and those regarding the conditions of the publication and the policing of the printing establishment.

The law that the government is proposing to the legislative body concerns neither the repression nor the conditions of the publication; it is only concerned with the right to judge a cause.

It is therefore indispensable that we indicate to you in what spirit you can apply the resolution, which, having an essentially political

35. Daumier register.
36. Collins, 161.
37. This document was brought to my attention by Nicole Brondel who kindly e-mailed me a scan of the circular.

character, must, as long as it remains in force, be adapted to the fundamental principles which preside in all our conduct. These are just general indications. *You must determine yourself, in each particular case, the opinion that seems to you the most wise.*

. . . it is not a question of the liberty of the human spirit nor of the rights of conscience, but simply of good faith and loyalty in respect to the law. (Emphasis mine)

But he goes on to write at the end of this letter, "You must not hesitate, if it becomes necessary, to seize upon the existent jurisdiction."

Two other *portraits-charges* appear in 1869: Adolphe Crémieux, the liberal representative who was elected deputy of Paris in 1869, is depicted shaking hands with François Arago, who died in 1853, and who was the astronomer of the Royal Observatory, a Republican opposed to Napoleon III, recalling "Twenty years after" (6 December, D. 3750). In "The return of Banquo-Glais-Bizon. When seeing him, the speaker, out of fear of being interrupted, interrupts his speech" (14 December, D. 3753); the reappearance of an old Republican of 1848 at the Assembly causes consternation. Bizon, with his deeply shaded eyes, is a powerful presence. By contrast, the orator with bulging eyes looks shocked; the violence of his reaction is indicated by his swept back hair. Daumier returns here to an earlier stylistic convention of large heads on small bodies.

Of the 75 Daumier lithographs published in 1870, 66 concern France, and 7, Prussia. The first few caricatures of the year are *portraits-charges*, such as in "Newly elected members of the Assembly preparing for a fight" (13 January D. 3758). Again using large heads and small bodies, Daumier caricatures Cremieux, Gambetta, deputy from 1869–70, who was a member of the National Defense and proclaimed the Republic on September 4, and Rochefort, a politician and journalist.

Daumier shows Thiers as a prompter at the theater—a metaphor for his role in French politics (7 February, D. 3764). In "The Statue of Silence" (15 February, D. 3767) lightly draped in a Roman toga, Thiers wears an elusive expression: he appears on a pedestal (modeled on a sculpture by Préault) surrounded by men looking up quizzically. The subtitle makes reference to the Nymph Egeria of Roman mythology, who was consulted by her king to whom she gave medical advice. Thiers opposed the war with Prussia but was vindicated after the defeat. He urged peace negotiations. In 1871 he became the President of the Republic.

The press is the subject of "Yoohoo, here it is again!" A man in a kiosk holds up a newspaper marked *"La Liberté"* to a bystander, who reacts with surprise (12 March, D. 3770).[38] Pressure on the press is the subject of "Will she be helped enough . . ." in which an older female figure representing the press is burdened by a large sack marked "tax on advertisements," while the stamp tax is being carried off in another large bag (17 June, D. 3790).

After Louis Napoleon declared war on Prussia on July 19, 1870, Daumier focused on the calling up of the reserves. Armed men march by a cropped pedestal marked France, with the caption, "Those who are about to die, salute thee" (2 September, D. 3804). On the day it was published, Bismarck's army was victorious in the Battle of Sedan. Napoleon III was captured and abdicated, marking the end of the Second Empire. Daumier drew allegorical scenes of France suffering.

The exercise of censorship then altered significantly and the functions of the bookstores and the press changed. Publishers no longer had to register caricatures in advance and the warrants were abolished on September 10. However, the situation did not become stable until 1872. Laharie notes that the Direction of the Press was suppressed on September 29, 1870, and replaced by a special office in the Bureau of Publicity, which reported to the Director General of Personnel. The press profited from this change of administrative oversight.[39]

On September 4, 1870, Paris workers invaded the Bourbon Palace calling for the fall of the Empire and declaring the Third Republic. Daumier depicts a cryptic summary of the career of Napoleon III in "History of a Reign" (12 September, D. 3808). The allegorical figure of France, bound, stands between two cannons, one marked "Paris 1851," alluding to the plebiscite under Napoleonic pressure, and the other marked "1870 Sedan." "The Republic calls us! Let us be victorious or die" (20 September, D. 3810) depicts an older man with rifle on his shoulder, kissing his little child goodbye as he marches off to war.

The Government of National Defense abolished the stamp duty on September 5 that same year, and the caution money a month later.[40]

---

38. This image also appeared on April 6, 1866.
39. Brondel, e-mail of 8 August 2010.
40. Laharie, xiii.

The Register of Documents of the Division of the Press and Printing of the Ministry of the Interior indicates that despite the decree of September 10, 1870, which proclaimed the freedom of the press, the requirement to submit drawings for authorization continued to be applied according to the decree of February 17, 1852. While some freedom of the press was granted it was curtailed again during the state of siege by the German armies, which began on September 19.[41] With the occupation, the key issues regarding censorship, such as trial by jury and a new libel law, had to wait for the war's end and a new parliament.[42] However, a decree of October 10 abolished the caution money and that of October 27 submitted the offenses of the press to the jurisdiction of a jury.[43]

When the government of the National Defense started negotiating with the Prussians, the workers revolted. In "L'Empire, c'est la paix" (The Empire means peace), the motto of Napoleon III (19 October 1870, D. 3814, Fig. 6), Daumier draws corpses in the street before the smoking ruins of houses. "Page of History" (16 November D. 3820) pictures a dead eagle crushed by Victor Hugo's volume *Les châtiments* (The Chastisements, 1852) that prophesied the fall of Napoleon III. Wounded France is pushed by a Prussian at gun point to the electoral urn in a caricature with the caption "What certain newspapers would call a free election" (24 November 1870, D.3823). The invading German troops had been putting pressure on the French transitional government to have an election in Paris.[44]

Sixty-four caricatures by Daumier were published in *Le charivari* in 1871, 50 are about France, 9 Germany, and 5 others deal with European subjects. The aftermath of the siege is the key subject. In "Dismayed with her heritage" (January 11, D. 3838), the mother of the country looks in despair at the devastation caused by the war. The five months of siege resulted in a terrible famine. On January 28, 1871, Paris surrendered to the Prussians. On February 1, Daumier published the powerful image of a blasted tree—"Poor France . . . the trunk has been struck by lightning" (D. 3843). The February 3 issue

41. See Archives nationales, F 18, *Déclaration des imprimeurs et libraires sous le régime du décret du 10 septembre 1870.*

42. *Ibid.*

43. Pierre Albert, "La presse française de 1871–1940," in *Histoire générale de la presse française*, ed. Claude Bélanger et. al., volume 3, 151.

44. Daumier register.

L'Empire c'est la paix.

Figure 6. Honoré Daumier, "The Empire Means Peace." *Le charivari*, October 19, 1870. (D. 3814) Benjamin A. and Julia M. Trustman Collection of Honoré Daumier Lithographs. Robert D. Farber University Archives and Special Collections Department, Brandeis University.

of *Le charivari* includes Daumier's drawing of the female figure of France dead on the battlefield (D. 3844). Ten lithographs by Daumier published in *Le charivari* appeared as well in the *Album du Siège* containing 40 images issued during the Commune. It was a promotional endeavor by the editor to offset the steep decline of subscriptions because of the war.

Daumier's caricatures attacked the new government in Versailles, elected on February 8, 1871. He recalls the plebiscite of May 1870, which ultimately resulted in the war with Prussia. "These killed that" (February 9, D. 3845) shows the figure of France, angry, older, disheveled, hair loosened as in mourning, pointing to the urn with its "yes" votes. With her other hand, she points to the field of corpses behind her.

In the elections of February 1871, the monarchists and conservatives outnumbered the Left, two to one, and nominated Thiers as Chief of the Executive Power. Issues concerning the press continued. Because the Tribunals were so unpopular, their verdicts regarding the press caused public outcry. The conservative government backed trials by jury, arguing that their verdicts would have the support of public opinion to put an end to the violence raging in the press.[45] Thiers actually supported protecting the moderate Republican press, as a counter balance to the persistent demands of the monarchists.[46] Daumier was able to continue with his domestic political caricature. "France-Prometheus and the eagle vulture" (13 February, D. 3847) shows France pinned to a rock, her liver attacked by a vulture.

The metaphor of theater and performance appears on February 24 (D. 3850): Thiers appears on the stage with Prussia in the background, his foot on a dead female figure, probably representing France. "The Assembly of Bordeaux, a conciliatory attitude of those who are called the moderate party" (11 March, D. 3855) shows three figures with, respectively, expressions of panic, outrage, and resignation.

The press law under the Commune (March 18, 1871 to May 28, 1871) left the section dealing with censorship of caricature untouched: 1870–71 witnessed a very harsh and arbitrary exercise of censorship.[47] The Commune struck the press with increasing severity, closing many of the newspapers.[48] This may explain why *Le charivari* was

45. Collins, 165.
46. Albert, 15.
47. Goldstein, 201–2.
48. Guiral, 375

suspended from April 22 to June 20. During the Commune, Daumier published only nine caricatures, the first appearing on March 30: Paris, a crowned female, pushes a recoiling representative to look at a field of graves, with the caption, "See M. Réac, it is quite enough" (D. 3858). Here a real figure is juxtaposed with an allegorical one: her strong figure, graceful pose, and calm face contrasted with his portly, awkward body and fearful expression. On April 1, Daumier depicted a worker standing before the ruins of his house. The caption reads, "It was not for this that I voted yes" (D. 3859).

Unlike some of his contemporaries, Daumier did not caricature any of the women who participated in the Commune, from the mothers and daughters who brought food and arms to the infamous working class *petroleuses*. Rather, he shows the conflict between classes and the betrayal of the politicians.

In April, with the help of the Prussians, the French army bombarded Paris. By the end of May 1871, the barricades were dismantled and the National Guard defeated. Some 30,000 communards were killed. Images of death and destruction prevail in Daumier's drawings of Paris and France, defeated.

But with the failure of the Commune, which had seen a temporary flourishing of Republican and revolutionary journals during the Third Republic, the trials against the press continued.[49] The law of 15 April 1871 indicates that there were still considerable restrictions on the press that carried over from 1849, "relative to the pursuit and exercise of offensive material by the press." In summary: Article 1—the pursuit of offensive material—still follows the laws of 1819 and 27 July 1849 with the following exceptions. Article 2 – the correctional tribunals continue to recognize: 1) the offenses committed against customs and manners (*moeurs*) by the publication, display, distribution, or sale of drawings, prints, lithographs, paintings, and emblems; 2) the offense of defamation and public injury concerning the personal (*particuliers*); 3) the offenses of verbal injury against all people; 4) the purely material infractions of the law, decrees and regulations of the press.[50] However, the Assemblée nationale liberalized the 1852 decrees, stating that juries should replace the correctional tribunals in matters of the press, arguing that the criteria were difficult to apply as there was

49. Jean Pierre-Bloch, *Liberté et servitude de la presse en France* (Monte-Carlo : Éditions du livre, 1952).

50. *Le bulletin des lois*, Assemblée nationale.

a wide range of writers with very varied tones, and of institutions. In 1870, a writer notes: "It is the jury that finds the correct voice and the natural interest of opinion."[51]

While the laws of 1871 were rapidly voted in, ambivalence prevailed due to the instability and uncertainty regarding the institutions that led both sides to avoid a more explicit text regarding censorship. The conservatives preferred to remain ambiguous so as to manipulate the multiple repressive strictures that had not been repealed, and the Left hoped for an electoral success in the future that would give them a better chance for a greater liberal law. In the meantime, they would accept the compromise. The equivocal situation regarding censorship would prevail until 1879.[52] On July 8, 1871 a bill was passed, which was in effect until September 16, negating the decrees of October 10, 1870, re-imposing caution money and restraint of liberty of the press.[53] That summer, there was another shift: the Republicans won 100 of the 118 vacant seats in the Assemblée nationale.

But the hope of liberty and peace was short lived. Monarchists and reactionary efforts continued to challenge the government. "La République de Milo or the ideal of the Right," (16–17 August, D. 3873) shows an armless female allegorical figure with a shield marked Republic to her side. She shows no signs of her revolutionary origins: a group of nearly featureless men stand below looking up at her. "The hatchet which would cut it has not yet been tempered" (7 September, D. 3877) pictures the jester standing by a tree marked "universal suffrage." Thiers is shown straddling two rocks marked "left" and "right" in "The President of Rhodes," (12 September, D. 3878.) Infringements on the press appear in "That which some would call progress," showing a figure symbolizing the press in a stockade marked "Tax on Paper," with the one marked "stamp tax" empty.

The last year of Daumier's activity coincided with the establishment of the Third Republic. Thirty-six of his caricatures were published in *Le charivari* in 1872; all are political and all but three are about France. Many caricatures concern the elections. In "France prepares to measure her candidates," the figure of France is shown in charge, towering over the small men who react in surprise. Again

51. In L. Gabriel-Robinet, *La censure* (Paris : Hachette, 1965), 107.

52. Albert, 150.

53. Christophe Charle, *Le siècle de la presse, 1830–1939* (Paris : Éditions du Seuil, 2004), 360.

the monumental female figure representing the ideal is contrasted with the diminutive reality. The metaphor of theater is used with the audience protesting, calling out "Curtain" before the stage curtain marked *"Théâtre de politique,"* referring to the lack of seriousness Daumier perceived in the government (13 January, D. 3904). A number of caricatures concern the division of parliamentary support between Left and Right. Ratapoil, the agent provocateur of Napoleon III, whom he resembles, created as a type by Daumier in sculpture and caricature in 1850–51 as a symbol of the corrupt Right, aims his arrow at the allegorical figure of the Republic who stands on a high pedestal (February 26, D. 3909). The danger of the reactionaries takes another form when Thiers appears as a station-master unable to stop the oncoming train marked "Reac" (where it is cut off, for Reaction) (15 May, D. 3924).

"If the workers are fighting each other, how can the building be restored?" (17 May, D. 3925. Fig. 7), which appeared two days later, depicts two workers standing on top of ruins fighting each other. In one of Daumier's last caricatures, published on May 27 in the newspaper, *Le peuple souverain* (The Sovereign People), a massive electoral urn, representing the weight of the votes, is shown crushing fallen figures on the battlefield marked "Sedan" (D. 3928): Napoleon III represents the old Empire, the Count of Chambord, the Legitimist interest, and the Duke of Aumale, the Orléanist. The electoral urn stands for the general elections in the country. An old figure marked "Monarchy" approaches a worker: the caption reads "Thank you old one, you're too decrepit" (8 June, D. 3931). Three representatives with long noses are shown asleep in "View taken from the Right," (D. 3934) which was published on June 28, 1871, when 160 deputies of the center Right played a leading role in the Assemblée nationale.

In Daumier's last published lithograph, "And they keep saying she has never been better" (September 24, 1872, D. 3937), a female figure representing the monarchy lies dead in a coffin, set against a black background. While the monarch had not been allowed to be represented, his symbol lies buried, at last.

Daumier essentially ceased doing caricatures at this point; his vision had been failing and he was going blind. In three periods of his life as a caricaturist, 1830–1835, 1848–1851, and 1866–1872, when not utterly prohibited by the censorship laws and their enforcement, Honoré Daumier drew the most powerful and effective images of

Figure 7. Honoré Daumier, "If the workers are fighting each other, how can the building be restored?" *Le charivari*, May 17, 1872 (D. 3925) Benjamin A. and Julia M. Trustman Collection of Honoré Daumier Lithographs. Robert D. Farber University Archives and Special Collections Department, Brandeis University.

French and European political issues with a profound moral force and masterful style. He developed the use of allegory in caricature as a means of subversion, by suggestion and imagination, in both subject and style, turning indirection into direction, and so challenging the constraints imposed by censorship.

BERTRAND TILLIER

The Impact of Censorship on Painting and Sculpture, 1851–1914

In the strictest legal sense, censorship has not existed in France since 1830, and certainly not since the passage of the law of 29 July 1881 liberalizing public expression. If censorship is taken to include nothing short of advance political vetting of every form of public expression, such later measures as seizure or prohibition, even destruction and penal judgments, though imposed strictly in accordance with the laws in force, do not qualify as censorship in its full repressive sense. De facto, however, by means of decrees, laws, orders or statutes, censorship was exercised continually – irrespective of the régime in power, be it authoritarian, conservative or liberal, and often with little variation—from the end of the Second Republic to the eve of World War I: under the Second Empire, during the Paris Commune of 1871, and even under the Third Republic, apropos of which Jean-Yves Mollier has pointed out that with respect to the press the régime was "often notable for the very excesses for which its proponents had condemned the Empire prior to 1870."[1]

With regard to the visual arts, censorship focused above all, throughout the second half of the nineteenth century, on caricature and the satirical press, on photography and photomontage—a sphere whose history is deserving of study in its own right. But painting, engraving, sculpture, and public monuments and emblems were also subject to retributive measures. This is a chapter in the history of art in modern France that is still little known if not disparaged, perhaps because it is so tightly bound up with the political history of

---

1. Jean-Yves Mollier, "La survie de la censure d'État (1881–1949)," in *La censure en France*, ed. Pascal Ory (Brussels: Complexe, 1997), 82. Translations throughout are by the translator.

YFS 122, *Out of Sight: Political Censorship of the Visual Arts in Nineteenth-Century France*, ed. Goldstein, © 2012 by Yale University.

artistic institutions and with the social history of taste and its periodic esthetic scandals. The repeated and often spectacular refusals by Salon juries that punctuate the history of modern art have indeed long seemed like a barely concealed chronicle of censorship, if not always of the political kind. Moreover, the historiography of post-Revolutionary France has tended to support the notion of a liberal policy toward art, laying much stress, for example, on the enlightened attitude implied by Napoleon III's authorization of the Salon des Refusés in 1863, or citing the forceful declarations of Republican élites in favor of a free art in a free State.[2]

The fact remains that between 1850 and 1914 harsh political censorship was regularly applied to artists and to specific works. It is the history of these repressive measures, at once disturbing and almost impossible to circumscribe, that I wish to describe in what follows, treating the issue, over and above changing political régimes, as a legislative continuum characteristic of this long and agitated period. I propose to discuss the means whereby censorship was employed, its motivations and applications, its active forms with respect to works and their authors, the places where it was practiced, and the resistance and strategies that it sometimes catalyzed among artists. From the application of judicial or police measures to more or less official acts of what can only be described as vandalism, the political censorship of works of art is also worthy of attention inasmuch as it betrays an archaic belief in the baneful effect of public imagery, a belief that still exerts an influence under modern conditions.

SYSTEMS OF JUDICIAL CENSORSHIP

During the Second Empire, despite the increased permissiveness of the last, liberal years of the régime, and until its abrogation by a decree of 30 March 1870, the administration of public expression was subject to an organic decree of 17 February 1852, itself referring back to a law of 31 March 1820:

> No drawings, engravings, lithographs, medallions, prints, or emblems of any kind may be published, displayed, or sold without the prior authorization of the Ministry of the Police of Paris or the prefects of the departments. In the event of violation, the drawings, prints, engravings, lithographs, medallions, and emblems will be confiscated

2. Pierre Vaisse, *La Troisième République et les peintres* (Paris: Flammarion, 1995), 53ff.

by the courts of correction [i.e. magistrate sitting without a jury] and those who published them sentenced to a prison term of one month to a year, and a fine of 100 to 1000 Francs.

With the fall of the Empire and the proclamation of the Republic on 4 September 1870, freedom of expression was bolstered, but then, during the spring of 1871, for symmetrical reasons, both the Paris Commune and the Versaillese authorities reversed course in an attempt to stifle the propaganda of their respective adversaries.[3] After the Commune had been crushed, as images sympathetic to that revolution began to make their appearance,[4] a decree was issued on 28 December 1871, at the initiative of the military governor of Paris, General de Ladmirault, prohibiting the distribution of any representation of the Commune except for images of Paris in ruins and portraits of insurgents bearing the stamp of the minister of the interior, who granted a special authorization to chosen photographers, notably to E. Appert[5] and, though in a less generous form, to Pierre Petit.[6] This measure, originally applicable only in Paris, was later extended, by virtue of a new decree dated 25 November 1872, to every department in France, the aim being to arrest the widening distribution of images which people had begun to collect:

> The display, selling or hawking of any drawings, photographs or emblems liable to disturb the public peace is prohibited. In particular, all portraits of individuals prosecuted or convicted for their participation in the recent insurrectionary events are forbidden.[7]

Invoking the state of siege, which remained officially in force in the Seine department until September 1873, this legislation was implemented to the full and later added by the Republic of Moral Order to the judicial arsenal of measures of censorship directed against the distribution of newspapers, pamphlets, books, placards, songs, mementos, and images of all kinds by booksellers, peddlers, and hawkers.[8]

3. Robert Tombs, *La guerre contre Paris, 1871* (Paris: Aubier, 1997).

4. Bertrand Tillier, *La Commune de Paris, révolution sans images? Politique et représentations dans la France républicaine (1871–1914)* (Seyssel: Champ Vallon, 2004).

5. Stéphanie Sotteau Soualle, "Appert, photographe parisien (1860–1890): Atelier et actualité" (doctoral thesis in art history, Université Paris-IV Sorbonne, 2010).

6. See the exhibition catalogue *La Commune photographiée*, ed. Quentin Bajac (Paris: Musée d'Orsay, 2000).

7. Cited in André Rouillé, *La photographie en France, 1816–1871* (Paris: Macula, 1989), 485.

8. Mollier, *Le camelot et la rue. Polémique et démocratie au tournant des XIXᵉ et XXᵉ siècles* (Paris: Fayard, 2004).

On the basis of a system very similar to that introduced during the Second Empire, censorship was applied from the early years of the conservative Third Republic—thanks notably to the subjection of certain offenses to short prison terms by summary judgment (*correctionnelisation*) and to anti-hawking measures antedating the amnesty of 24 February 1878.[9] These practices continued until the great liberal law of 29 July 1881 superseded more than three hundred articles scattered among forty-two earlier laws, decrees, and orders. The liberalism of Republican lawmakers was not absolute, however.[10] In the first place, direct incitement to crimes and misdemeanors, calls for military disobedience, and offences against French or foreign heads of state all continued to be punishable acts. In addition, and despite a few vain attempts to buttress censorship, notably the legislation on insult and injury to individuals (*offenses et outrages aux personnes*) proposed by Marcel Barthe on 3 December 1889, significant restrictions were in fact introduced in three instances: the law of 2 August 1882[11] against public indecency (*outrage aux bonnes mœurs*); the referral to summary judgment of insults to foreign heads of state and diplomats (law of 16 March 1893); and the criminalization of anarchist propaganda (the *lois scélérates*, or "villainous laws," of 12 December 1893 and 28 July 1894).

All these legislative and judicial measures, more or less strictly enforced according to the period and the régime in power, together constituted the tool by means of which, during the second half of the nineteenth century and up until World War I, censorship was applied not only to such visual items as satirical images and photographs and their derivatives[12] but also to works of art proper.

VANDALISM AS CENSORSHIP

Beyond such institutional censorship, backed up by law, we should also consider the retributive removal, replacement, or modification

9. Christophe Charle, *Le siècle de la presse (1830–1939)* (Paris, Seuil, 2004), 133.

10. Jean-Pierre Machelon, *La République contre les libertés? Les restrictions aux libertés publiques de 1879 à 1914* (Paris: Fondation Nationale des Sciences Politiques, 1976).

11. Annie Stora-Lamarre, *L'enfer de la IIIᵉ République: Censeurs et pornographes (1881–1914)* (Paris: Imago, 1990), 179ff.

12. Robert Goldstein, *Censorship of Political Caricature in Nineteenth-Century France* (Kent, OH: Kent State University Press, 1989); Donald English, *Political Uses of Photography in the Third Republic: France, 1871–1914* (Ann Arbor: University of Michigan Press, 1984).

of public images by virtue of the more or less spontaneous, more or less organized actions that characterize times of political transition and are closely related to the tradition of revolutionary vandalism. In his plea in defense of Courbet, who had been accused of destroying the Vendôme Column,[13] the Republican Jules Castagnary, wishing to secure the painter's legacy in a symbolic way, recalled the obvious fact that:

> When a dynasty is overthrown, it is simple logic that its emblems should disappear along with it: on days of insurrection, therefore, some kinds of destruction are permitted, not to say obligatory. The fourth of September 1870 cannot be seen as different in this respect from either 29 July 1830 or 24 February 1848.[14]

Actions of this sort may also be described as a form of visual censorship somewhere between the extreme application of a political program and anarchic popular action. "In memory," Castagnary goes on,

> I can still see the National Guardsmen on the steps of the besieged legislative body ripping the eagles from their shakoes and throwing them to the ground, and the crowd applauding. These first actions were too banal to calm the people's frustration [and] fury towards the criminal author of the war [Napoleon III] merely redoubled. The idea that his image . . . should remain in place on our town squares, at our crossroads, on the façades of our public monuments, became impossible to contemplate. The authorities sensed the danger of excesses. They realized that to avert them the movement must be channeled and . . . that they must take the leadership. It was at their orders that the bas-relief by Barye [1866–68] representing Napoléon III on horseback was detached from its tympanum above the entrance of the Carrousel triumphal arch in Paris and exiled to storage; that Seurre's Napoleon in a grey frock-coat which had stood at the Courbevoie traffic circle was transported by night to the Pont de Neuilly and tossed into the Seine; and that Prince Eugène de Beauharnais was removed from his pedestal and replaced by a statue of Voltaire.[15]

Gestures of this sort, typical during the often fraught institution of new political orders, could also occur during times of civil war or heightened tension. Thus, some forty years on, the Communard

---

13. Jules Castagnary, *Gustave Courbet et la Colonne Vendôme*, ed. Bertrand Tillier (Tusson: Éditions Du Lérot, 2000 [1883]).

14. Ibid., 28.

15. Ibid., 28–29.

Maxime Vuillaume recalled visiting the Ministry of Justice on Place Vendôme and discovering a small Bosio bronze of Henri IV as a child. The figure had been thrust "head first" into the ground with its "legs sticking up in the air." "When you examined it closely," Vuillaume writes, "you noticed that the statue bore puncture wounds in a dozen or so places." He then recounts how some Fédérés, the day after the events of 18 March 1871, had set the statue up at the entrance to the ministry and fired their rifles at it, "laughing."[16] Similar acts of iconoclastic censorship were performed under the Third Republic in the wake of the Dreyfus Affair and directed notably at the "Dreyfus monuments"[17]—statues erected at the beginning of the twentieth century to honor such figures as Scheurer-Kestner, Ludovic Trarieux, Waldeck-Rousseau (Paris), Émile Zola (Suresnes), and Bernard Lazare (Nîmes), which were variously defaced, damaged, or defiled by the royalist Camelots du Roi of the Action Française movement under the leadership of the sculptor Maxime Réal del Sarte. What these activists called their "statue mission"[18] was driven by a desire to rectify—to correct in all senses of the term—what they viewed as the fraud embodied in these marble or bronze figures; they even planned to blow them up with the help of a chemist who had embraced their nationalist and anti-Dreyfusard ideas.[19] In this way the militant iconoclasts of Action Française gave public expression to their opinions; more than that, however, they felt they could control public space by exercising a form of censorship over images displayed there. Just like official censors, they were haunted by the fear that public and political space could be perverted. This fear was likewise the basis of actions taken against items as humdrum as hawkers' medallions, cufflinks, pipes or tobacco jars – actions whose niggling surveillance,

---

16. Maxime Vuillaume, *Mes cahiers rouges au temps de la Commune* [1909–1911], ed. Gérard Guégan (Arles: Actes Sud/Babel, 1998), 233.

17. The term used by Louis Dimier in *Vingt ans d'Action française et autres souvenirs* (Paris: Nouvelle Librairie Nationale, 1926), 118.

18. Police report of 20 February 1909, Archives de la Préfecture de Police de Paris, B/A 1342.

19. See Neil McWilliam, "Commemoration and the Politics of Iconoclasm: The Battle over 'Les statues Dreyfusardes,' 1908–1910," in *Memory and Oblivion: Proceedings of the 29th International Congress of the History of Art Held in Amsterdam, 1996*, ed. Wessel Reinink and Jeroel Stumpel (Amsterdam: Kluwer Academic Publishers, 1999), 581–86; and Tillier, *Les artistes et l'affaire Dreyfus (1898–1908)* (Seyssel: Champ Vallon, 2009), 291–312.

countless confiscations and destructions Fernand Drujon sought to record.[20]

POLITICAL MOTIVATIONS

In its institutional forms as in its more brutal ones, the censorship of imagery concorded with the political motivations of régimes that, in order to impose their legitimacy or values, needed to combat the iconic representations and references of their predecessors. We know that shortly after the coup d'état Prince-President Louis-Napoléon Bonaparte visited the Casimir Périer room in the Palais-Bourbon and had Jean-Auguste Barre's bust of "La République" from 1848 replaced by his own portrait. A month later, by a decree dated 3 January 1852, coinage and postage stamps were changed, the personification of the Republic once again giving way to that of the future Napoleon III.[21] Censorship by way of substitution affected a great number of objects, images, and emblems: in many town halls busts of the Emperor supplanted those of the Republic, while the imperial eagle ousted the liberal cock and the Republican fasces. But the Empire also sought, more discreetly, to modify public iconography in more subtle ways. The sculptor Jean-François Soitoux would later recount that in 1864 the director of the École des Beaux-Arts urged him to retouch his monumental *République* of 1848, adding attributes of Justice or Liberty that would make it possible to install the work in a public space; the artist refused,[22] thus frustrating an attempt to debase the work in order to send a political message to the Republican opposition.

To ensure their stability the political régimes of the second half of the nineteenth century frequently resorted to the censorship of images. During the 1870s, for example, the conservative Third Republic used it to target not only references of a revolutionary kind but also to Bonapartist imagery. As Maurice Agulhon notes, in 1873 a circular of the Prefecture of the Var department required busts of Marianne wearing the Phrygian cap, too closely identified with the

20. Fernand Drujon, *Catalogue des ouvrages écrits et dessins de toute nature poursuivis, supprimés ou condamnés depuis le 21 octobre 1814 jusqu'au 31 juillet 1877* (Paris: Rouveyre, 1879).

21. Maurice Agulhon, *Marianne au combat. L'imagerie et la symbolique républicaines de 1789 à 1880* (Paris : Flammarion, 1979), 158.

22. Jacques Lethève, "Une statue malchanceuse: La République de Soitoux," *GBA* (October 1963), 229–40.

memories of 1793 and 1871, to be removed from town halls, with failure to comply meaning the unseating of the municipal council.[23] In Dijon, a Republican municipality had commissioned a monument from the sculptor Paul Cabet to commemorate the town's resistance to the Prussian invasion of autumn 1870. Cabet produced a Marianne wearing a Phrygian cap, whereupon, by prefectural order, the Mac-Mahon government ruled that this Trente-Octobre monument must be taken down—which was done in October 1875[24]—on account of its "revolutionary character."[25] But though the Republic thus censored images considered too radical, it also sought to prohibit the tens of thousands of portraits of Prince Louis—*images d'Épinal*, photographs, medallions, engravings, lithographs and the like peddled in Paris and throughout the provinces by former soldiers and functionaries of the Empire, on market stalls and even in schools—by means of whose dissemination the Bonapartists hoped to popularize the figure of Napoleon III after his early death in 1873. This surge of propaganda by image reached such proportions that on 4 February 1875 any and all distribution of representations of the future Napoleon IV was banned.[26]

The Republican Republic found itself obliged once again to resort to extralegal types of censorship during the Boulangist crisis, in order to counter the deployment of iconographic propaganda by General Boulanger, who had well understood the advantage he might gain from a heroic and bellicose imagery capable of arousing "the admiration of high and lowly alike for the person of Monsieur the Minister of War."[27] In March 1889 the Minister of the Interior ordered that all Boulangist documentary materials circulating within French territory—pamphlets, placards, posters, colored images—be confiscated; it was stressed that engraved portraits and photographs fell into the class of materials incriminated under these measures.[28] When Bou-

23. Agulhon, *Marianne au combat*, 194.
24. It would be restored on 30 October 1880, with the advent of the Republican Republic.
25. Chantal Martinet, "La République s'installe à Dijon: Histoire d'une bataille monumentale," *Les monuments historiques* 244 (April-May 1986); Laurent Baridon, "Le monument du Trente-Octobre 1870 à Dijon: Les malheurs d'une Marianne romantique," *Sources, travaux historiques* 26 (1991) : 13–23.
26. Bernard Ménager, *Les Napoléon du peuple* (Paris: Aubier, 1988), 292–95.
27. *Le Procès du Général Boulanger, Rochefort, Dillon, devant la Haute Cour de Justice* (Paris: Librairie Française, 1889), 71.
28. "Propagande boulangiste," 3 March 1889, Archives de la Préfecture de Police de Paris, BA/971.

langer came before the High Court of Justice, the Attorney General noted that "all these portraits sent into France had one ultimate purpose: they were intended to spread not enlightenment but merely the features of the General, the object undoubtedly being to precipitate demonstrations that would lead inexorably to a plebiscite."[29] At the Paris Universal Exposition in 1889, a portrait of General Boulanger painted by Édouard Debat-Ponsan, which had been exhibited at the Salon two years earlier, was taken down. The artist, feeling that the removal of the picture compromised the integrity of his consignment as a whole, refused the bronze medal that the jury awarded him in tribute to his work. After being removed, this equestrian portrait of Boulanger mounted on his thoroughbred disappeared—all that remains is a sketch (in a private collection) that was shown at the Tours Museum of Fine Arts in 1972[30]—but was perhaps sent to Belgium, where it is purported to have been displayed at traveling fairs after the General's spectacular suicide.

Especially between 1871 and 1914, the Third Republic also deployed censorship against images deemed liable to harm its diplomatic relations with other countries in the context of rising nationalisms and the Franco-German tensions revived by several crises, notably the Boulangist episode and the tortuous Dreyfus Affair. At the 1872 Salon, dubbed "the Salon of the Defeat," more than thirty works were initially offered to public view that evoked the events of 1870–1871, sometimes very directly, notably the war, the siege of Paris, and the loss of Alsace-Lorraine. But some of these were taken down, a move so dramatic that it attracted comment in the critical notices of both Zola and Castagnary. "By thus smothering the cry for vengeance against Prussia," wrote Zola, "the government has left us nothing but the gibbering of our pain."[31] Castagnary offered an explanation:

> a word about several paintings withdrawn from the Salon at the request of the Ministry . . . One morning Monsieur Charles Blanc called in the artists whose works, already accepted by the Salon and hung, dealt directly with the war. He told them that in view of pending negotiations Prussia now needed to be handled with the greatest prudence,

29. *Procès du Général Boulanger*, 74.

30. *Édouard Debat-Ponsan (1847–1913)*, exhibition catalogue, ed. Marie-Noëlle Pinot de Villechenon (Tours: Musée des Beaux-Arts, 1972).

31. Émile Zola, "Lettres parisiennes," *La cloche*, 12 May 1872; reprinted in *Écrits sur l'art* (Paris: Hermann, 1991), 258.

and he asked them to withdraw their entries. This was a sacrifice, but they all consented to it.[32]

In accordance with a directive from Thiers, all artists whose works depicted violent episodes of the recent war were indeed requested to withdraw them voluntarily from the Salon. Clearly the government feared that the public display of such works might compromise the progress of its negotiations with Von Arnim concerning the liberation of the territories occupied by German forces. In exchange for their patriotic sacrifice, the "solicited" artists received a letter of thanks of which a copy is still extant.[33] At least eight works were affected by this measure. They can be traced by virtue of the Salon's official catalog, which, once printed, was returned to the National Printing Office with instructions for the relevant sections to be reprinted with the mention of the excluded works deleted.[34] While those listings were removed, however, the numbering system was not modified. Dominique Lobstein,[35] who is reluctant to conclude that censorship occurred, has proposed the plausible hypothesis that the details of "withdrawn" works were deleted from the official catalog, and that they themselves were perhaps not on view at the Salon's opening, but that they were rehung ("were they quickly put back up," he wonders, "if in fact they had been taken down?") before the end of the exhibition, during which they were acquired by the State and photographs taken of them by Michelez for the album of State acquisitions.[36] Be that as it may, there can really be no doubt that some sort of censorship was applied to seven paintings and one sculpture representing scenes from the war of 1870.[37] And that by way of compensation, several of

---

32. Jules Castagnary, *Salons*, 2 vols. (Paris: Charpentier & Fasquelle, 1892), 2:35.

33. A copy of this circular letter is in the National Archives, Paris, F 21 492.

34. See *Le moniteur des arts*, 17 May 1872.

35. Dominique Lobstein, "1872: Un Salon désarmé?" *48/14, La Revue du Musée d'Orsay* 10 (Spring 2000) : 84–93.

36. The "Michelez" album of State acquisitions is at the Musée d'Orsay, Paris.

37. Following the numbering of the catalog of the 1872 Salon, the submissions withdrawn were the following, all in the Painting section: (3) *L'épisode de la bataille de Woerth*, a watercolor by Albert Adam; (72) *Triptyque*, a charcoal drawing by Émile Bayard; (507) *Un déménagement aux environs de Paris par l'armée prussienne*, by Édouard Detaille; (880) a work by Gustave Jundt; (1127) *Allégorie*, by Xavier-Alphonse Monchablon; (1428) *La Réquisition en Picardie*, by Louis Ulysse Souplet; and (1469) *Pillage d'une ferme par les Allemands*, by Benjamin Ulmann. For number (1839), neither work nor artist can be identified. As for the single work of sculpture, it may have been *Gisant de l'Abbé Miroy* (the parish priest of Cruchery, shot by the Prussians on 12 February 1871), a work commissioned by the Rheims municipality from the sculptor René de

these excluded works were bought by the State. Furthermore, some of the artists concerned received awards or honors: Édouard Detaille, for example, was granted a second-class medal at the 1842 Salon, while, in accordance with the honorific practices of the Beaux-Arts administration, Benjamin Ulmann was promoted to the rank of Chevalier de la Légion d'Honneur in the context of that same event. All these official acts bear witness to a desire to attenuate, if not indeed to conceal the censorship. A good number of newspapers concentrated for their part on some of the banned works, making every effort to describe them in the minutest detail—to the point, even, where the art actually on display at the Salon was paradoxically given less attention. They all underlined the starkness of the Detaille and Ulmann pictures, the one portraying a band of Prussian marauders leaving Paris after their depredations, the other showing Prussians pillaging a farm in the Alsatian countryside. Meanwhile, when Goupil, a publisher of engravings who displayed these two works in his Paris gallery until June 1872, requested permission to distribute photographic reproductions of them, his application was turned down on the basis of the legislation of 28 December 1871.[38]

On two other occasions works submitted to the Salon were targeted by political censorship stemming from government fears that diplomatic relations between France and Germany were jeopardized by them. Thus a monumental work by Benjamin Ulmann, *Thiers salué du titre de "Libérateur du territoire" le 16 juin 1877 à l'Assemblée nationale* (Thiers Hailed as "Liberator of the Territory" on 16 June 1877 by the National Assembly),[39] after being accepted by the 1877 Salon, was taken down and later returned to the artist. Twenty years later, Jean Veber encountered similar difficulties when, at the 1897 Salon of the Société Nationale des Beaux-Arts (SNBA), he exhibited a canvas of a satirical nature entitled *La boucherie* (Butchery), depicting Bismarck as a butcher flanked by two dogs—Francis Joseph of Austria on the left and Wilhelm II on the right—standing at a bloody counter laden with severed human heads.[40] In response to protests from the German embassy in Paris, the work was hastily

Saint-Marceaux, and which earned him a second-class medal (see the exhibition catalog *Une famille d'artistes en 1900: Les Saint-Marceaux* [Paris: Musée d'Orsay, 1992], 36–37.

38. Robert Allen Jay, *Art and Nationalism in France, 1870–1914* (doctoral dissertation, University of Minnesota, 1979), 29ff.

39. Oil on canvas, 1877, Musée Historique Lorrain, Nancy.

40. Oil on canvas, 1897, Jane Voorhees Zimmerli Art Museum, New Brunswick, NJ.

taken down and returned to the artist, who nevertheless produced a pastel version[41] and a lithograph that was widely distributed and went through several impressions from 1899 on.[42]

METHODS

The motives for censorship may have been few, but the methods available for its legal imposition on artists and their works were far more numerous and constitute a veritable preventive or repressive armamentarium. It may be useful to distinguish between measures taken against artists and those taken against works. Under the Second Empire and in the early days of the Third Republic, after his involvement in the Paris Commune, Courbet often complained—at times in a way that suggested fantasy or even delusion—of the surveillance and retribution to which he felt he was being subjected. In a letter of 1864 to Victor Hugo, which has a good measure of invention and exaggeration—features that may reasonably be viewed as reactions to real persecution—the painter writes as follows:

> When Delacroix and you were in your prime, you did not have, as I do, an Empire to say to you "Outside of us there is no salvation." There was no warrant for your arrest; your mothers, unlike mine, did not make underground passages in the house to hide you from the police; Delacroix never saw soldiers violating his home, erasing his paintings with a bucket of turpentine, by a minister's order; his works were not arbitrarily excluded from the Exhibition [the Salon]; . . . unlike me, he did not have that pack of mongrels howling at his heels. . . . The battles were about art . . . ; you were not threatened with banishment. The pigs tried to eat democratic art in its cradle, but in spite of everything democratic art is growing up and will eat them. In spite of the oppression that weighs on our generation, in spite of the fact that my friends are in exile, hunted down, even with dogs, in the Morvan forests, there are still four or five of us left. We are strong enough, despite the renegades, despite the France of today with its demented sheep. We will save art, the life of the mind, and integrity in our country.[43]

41. Pastel, ca. 1897–99, Musée des Beaux-Arts, Tours.
42. Richard Thomson, *The Troubled Republic: Visual Culture and The Social Debate in France, 1889–1900* (New Haven: Yale University Press, 2004).
43. Courbet to Hugo, 28 November 1864, *Letters of Gustave Courbet*, ed. and trans. Petra ten-Doesschate Chu (Chicago: University of Chicago Press, 1992), letter no. 64–18, 249.

Under the Republic, too, artists were placed under surveillance for political reasons. The archives of the Paris Prefecture of Police[44] contain a file on the battle painter Édouard Armand-Dumaresq, who was shadowed by the police in 1878 after buying a tricorn at the Hôtel Drouot auction house that was said to have been worn by Napoleon during his Russian campaign and put up for sale by the heir of the Emperor's valet and tailor.[45] In the eyes of the Republican authorities this act expressed a suspect fetishism betraying the artist's Bonapartist sympathies.

Measures against works rather than artists were nevertheless far more frequent and, though sporadic, far more numerous all through the second half of the nineteenth century. Statues were targeted—demolished or replaced, like that of Prince Eugène de Beauharnais, removed from its plinth in September 1870 and replaced by a statue of Voltaire, or like Cabet's female figure in the Phrygian cap in the Dijon Trente-Octobre monument. But it was above all the Salon, as a public exhibition space, that became the theater of every kind of tactic and machination designed to censor works of varying degrees of openness. Often acts of censorship were discreet, and hard to characterize inasmuch as the motivation for them jumbled up aesthetic and political considerations. The painter and press artist Adolphe Willette was censored on two occasions. At the 1886 Salon he had his picture "Israel and Co." refused. This work showed a locomotive driven by a Jew laying waste to everything in its path and leaving nothing but corpses in its wake, while a priest exhorted a motley crowd—a throng of judges, soldiers, proletarians, revolutionaries, vagabonds, and Bonapartists at the foot of a barricade – to resist the Jews' stranglehold on the country: "Sons of France, unite to destroy this abominable machine, or you are lost!"[46] The following year, 1887, it was the turn of another canvas of Willette's, entitled *La Sainte Démocratie*

---

44. Archives de la Préfecture de Police de Paris, BA/1059.

45. Sale of 1 August 1878, administered by Maître Maurice Véron, the official appraiser. A police report of the same date notes that the auction was held in the presence of "several well-known members of the Bonapartist party."

46. The picture has never been located. Willette made a graphic version of it that was published as a two-page spread in the *Courrier français* for 7 November 1886. Another version (or a rearranged version) was shown at the 1890 Salon under the title *La machine infernale* (item no. 828). See Laurent Bihl, "La grande mascarade parisienne" (doctoral thesis in history, Université Paris-1 Panthéon-Sorbonne, 2010), 787.

(Holy Democracy),[47] to be rejected by the Salon, while its reproduction on the front page of *Le courrier français* caused the offending issue to be confiscated from the newsstands.[48] The motives for this particular measure would seem to have been multiple, both political and moral, for the work was an explosive blend of anti-Republicanism and pornography.[49]

Censorship at the Salon was substantial and usually effective. In 1869, having exhibited nothing for years, Paul Chenavard sent in the monumental *Divina Tragedia*, a dramatic and complex work, rich in iconography and grey in tone.[50] Thanks to Casimir Périer, we have a clear idea of just what occurred in connection with this picture.[51] The anticlerical and freethinking Périer pays homage to a painter who "has set out to capture on canvas a great and poetic image"[52]—the image of the collapse of all religions, even Christianity—and salute "the dizzying hubbub, the inter-dogmacidal carnage and the downward plunge into the abyss of nothingness of all the wild, ridiculous or sublime delusions" of intolerant and superstitious faiths.[53] Périer goes on to describe the masked censorship brought to bear on this painting, which had to be hung in the Louvre's Salon Carré, where it could not effectively convey its anti-Christian message. The work was not refused, nor was it taken down. But in the publishing office of the Salon guide (Périer underscores the fact that the government was empowered to monitor the guide and sales stands), where the names and descriptions of works were registered, the original title, *La fin de toutes les religions et le triomphe de la Pensée libre* (The End of All Religions and the Triumph of Free Thought), was replaced by the Dantesque *Divina Tragedia*, while the picture's message was literally reversed in an ad hoc subtitle claiming that the subject was "The Triumph of the Christian Religion over Every Other Religion on Earth." In his account of the 1869 Salon, Périer reproduces a two-

47. The canvas is known only by way of a photograph (Bihl-Willette family collection).

48. Adolphe Willette, "Je suis la Sainte Démocratie: J'attends mes amants," *Le courrier français*, 11 December 1887.

49. See the valuable collection of documents in Bihl, "La grande mascarade," 535–40.

50. Oil on canvas, 1869, Musée d'Orsay, Paris.

51. Paul-Casimir Périer, "La commission de l'index à l'Exposition," in *Propos d'art à l'occasion du Salon de 1869: Revue du Salon* (Paris: Michel Lévy, 1869).

52. Ibid., 306.

53. Ibid., 308

column table presenting a term-by-term comparison of the manipulations to which Chenavard's work was subjected.[54]

At the start of the Third Republic, works associated with the Commune were either seized in advance to prevent their exhibition at the Salons or else rejected by the jury following unofficial intervention by the Beaux-Arts administration in accordance with political directives. At the 1875 Salon, for instance, two works evoking the Versaillese repression of the Commune were censored. Auguste Lepère saw his picture *Épisode de la Commune, rue des Rosiers à Montmartre*[55] rejected by the Salon jury. The painter had depicted the place where, during the *Semaine sanglante*, as a reprisal for the Communards' execution of General Clément Thomas and General Lecomte, shot on 18 March 1871, the Versaillese had massacred women and children residing on that street who were suspected of being supporters of the Commune. Lepère portrayed these victims being guarded by Versaillese soldiers as they awaited the firing squad.[56] In similar fashion, Ernest Pichio submitted to the Salon jury a picture entitled *Le triomphe de l'ordre*, or alternatively *Le mur des Fédérés*[57] (Figure 1), which offered a lyrical vision of the last executions at the Federals' Wall in the Père-Lachaise cemetery.[58] That work was intercepted by Marquis Philippe de Chennevières, chief administrator of the École des Beaux-Arts, who cautioned the artist in the following terms:

> Such painful memories should not be evoked in a national competition; they are by their nature liable to arouse political passions from which art must remain detached. I find myself in consequence obliged, after conferring with the Minister [of Public Education] to request you to have this picture withdrawn from the Palais des Champs-Élysées. It will be returned to you.[59]

As a rule it was the police who demanded that particular works be removed from exhibits that would expose them to public view. Many pictures in the Salon were taken down in this way, often despite a jury's initial acceptance of them. Not without hesitation, however, as Courbet noted with respect to the exclusion of his *Return from the*

54. Thomas Schlesser, *Paul Chenavard, Monuments de l'échec (1807–1895)* (Dijon: Presses du Réel, 2009), 183–91; Périer's picture is reproduced on 248–50.

55. Oil on canvas, 1875, Musée Carnavalet, Paris.

56. Tillier, *La Commune de Paris*, 254–55.

57. This work has been lost.

58. Tillier, *La Commune de Paris*, 255ff.

59. Letter of 24 mars 1875. Cited in ibid., 257.

Figure 1. Ernest Pichio, *Le triomphe de l'ordre*, also known as *Le mur des Fédérés*, circa 1875, print. Musée d'art et d'histoire de Saint Denis.

Conference (Figure 2) from the 1863 Salon: "The painting hit home, it went straight to its author. It has been taken down and rehung three or four times. If one were to talk to Walewski,[60] it could perhaps be rehung a fifth time."[61] In 1891, the Minister of the Interior demanded the withdrawal of a picture by René Vauquelin hung at the Salon de la Société des Artistes Français (SAF). Entitled *Finis coronat opus*, this work showed human skulls in the middle of a desert, one of them being that of Jules Ferry, at which a crow was starting to peck.[62] The 1908 SNBA Salon witnessed several measures of this kind, motivated by the consequences of the Dreyfus Affair. The sculptor and anti-Dreyfusard Jean Baffier[63] included in his submissions the original plaster cast of a monumental medallion produced on a subscription basis several months earlier by the Action Française movement to commemorate General Mercier's speech before the Senate (Figure 3) contesting to Dreyfus's reinstatement in the army. In February 1908, in an attempt to forestall a possible refusal, Baffier had gone to see the SNBA president, painter Alfred Roll, a man well known for his Republican and Deyfusard convictions. Doubtless in order to deprive nationalists of an opportunity to portray themselves as victims of censorship, the SNBA committee assented to Baffier's showing this work, albeit, in view of the passionate reactions that it was liable to stir up, entirely "at his own risk." Two days before the Salon's official opening by its president, Armand Fallières, on 13 April 1908, the sculptor set up his medallion in a display case specially designed so that the inscriptions on both faces could be read. On the obverse, crowning Mercier's profile, ran the violent dedication "To General Mercier bringer of justice to the traitor Dreyfus—National Subscription"; the reverse bore the clearest statement from Mercier's Senate declaration: "The conviction I formed during the debates of 1899 has not altered in the slightest. My conscience forbids me to vote for the motion you are about to propose." After making an inspection, however, police officials ordered Baffier to withdraw his medallion from the Salon, and at the same time instructed two painters, Paul

60. The natural son of Napoleon I, Alexandre Walewski was Minister of State in charge of the administration of fine arts.

61. Courbet to Albert de la Fizière, 23 April 1863, *Letters of Gustave Courbet*, no. 63–69, 221.

62. See *La nation*, 30 May 1891; and Archives nationales, Paris, F 21 4086.

63. Neil McWilliam, *Monumental Intolerance: Jean Baffier, A Nationalist Sculptor in Fin-de-Siècle France* (Philadelphia: Pennsylvania State University Press, 2000).

Figure 2. Gustave Courbet, *Le retour de la conférence*, oil on canvas, 1863, destroyed.

Figure 3. Jean Baffier, Advertisement for the *Médaille au général Mercier* in *L'action francaise*, April 15, 1908.

Renouard and Jean Veber, to take their works down. Whereas Veber's entry, entitled *Vision d'Allemagne, Circuit du Taunus* (Vision of Germany – The Taunus Circuit) and directed against Wilhelm II, threatened to worsen already tense diplomatic relations between France and Germany, the Renouard work also referred to Dreyfus. Renouard, who had taken part in the Rennes trial as a court artist, was submitting a painting entitled *La Vision (Rennes, août 1899)* depicting the protagonists of the court martial as they waited for a session to open. Recognizable phantoms blended into the scene: guilty of spying, Ferdinand Walsin Esterhazy could be seen bringing the dead body of Lieutenant-Colonel Henry—forger of the documents that made it possible for Dreyfus to be found guilty—to Mercier, thus incriminating the general as an accomplice in Henry's murder, which had been disguised as a suicide. Renouard's work was an unambiguous denunciation, clearly identifying the guilty parties and amounting to a further declaration of Dreyfus's innocence. The order to take the picture down sprang from a wish to avoid fueling nationalist ire. A precise description of the painting was nevertheless given in the press by a journalist who demanded to know "why they wish to prevent this great tableau, so impressive and of such meticulous artistry, from sounding its so very timely note of truth, morality and history?"[64] The impeached work was eventually rehung at the Salon, but only after the printer agreed to remove the legend, which referred explicitly to Henry's suicide: "Everyone expected it: some hoped for it, others feared it." For his part, Baffier was invited by the SNBA committee to show his medallion with its inscriptions expurgated; this he declined to do, choosing to claim that his work was the sole victim of government censorship zealously enforced by Lépine, the prefect of police.[65]

Political prohibitions on the public showing of a work or the decision to withdraw one from display were often followed by further measures targeting the production and distribution of reproductions. Thus in 1867 the police destroyed reproductions of Courbet's painting *Return from the Conference* (1863) at the studio of the photographer Bingham;[66] and in February 1876 photographs of the illustrations in his anticlerical pamphlet *Les curés en goguette* (Priests in their Cups), published in Brussels in 1868—and once again, notably, of the 1863 work—were impounded at a Paris bookseller's.[67] Manet too ran into censorship when he tried to publish a lithograph of a painting he was intending to submit to the 1869 Salon, namely *L'exécution de Maximilien* (Figure 4), which evoked the death of the Emperor of Mexico, shot by revolutionaries in 1867 after Napoleon III withdrew the support of French troops. After submitting a proof to the appropriate bureau of the Ministry of the Interior, Manet was forbidden to proceed with his plans for printing and distribution, this doubtless because the uniforms of the firing squad as portrayed too closely resembled those of Imperial Guard's *chasseurs à pied*, and the administration therefore suspected the painter of wishing to implicate

64. Flammèche, "Un tableau sur l'Affaire," *L'action*, 15 April 1908.

65. Tillier, *Les artistes et l'affaire Dreyfus (1898–1908)* (Seyssel: Champ Vallon, 2009), 285–88.

66. Courbet to Castagnary, 21 April 1867, *Letters of Gustave Courbet*, no. 67–69, 310.

67. Drujon, *Catalogue* (see n. 20), 114.

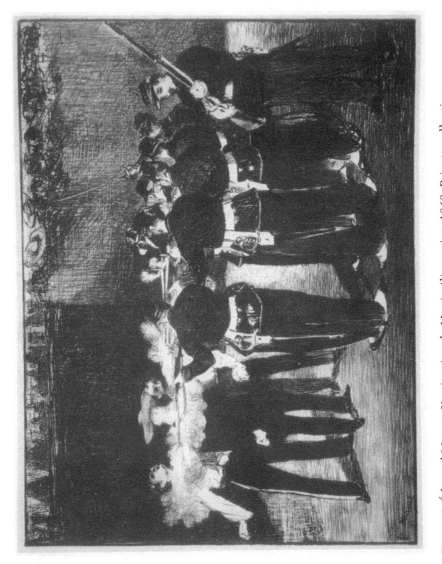

Figure 4. Édouard Manet, *L'exécution de Maximilien*, print, 1869. Private collection.

Napoleon III in the death of Maximilian of Austria at a time when the Republican opposition was interpreting this execution as an exemplification of the dithering and inconsistency of the Empire's foreign policy. Hence Manet received a letter putting him on notice that his painting could not be shown in the Salon and that the distribution of prints would no longer be authorized.[68] In the mid-1870s, Ernest Pichio was subjected to a similar ban on reproductions of two of his pictures that were critical of the Versaillese repression of the Commune, namely *Le triomphe de l'ordre* and *La veuve du fusillé* (The Widow of the Executed Man),[69] refused by the Salons of 1875 and 1877 respectively. Pichio was not granted the necessary peddler's license and was thus unable to distribute reproductions of his works, which he had intended to print as color-tinted photographs.

ARTISTS' STRATEGIES OF RESISTANCE

Faced by acts of censorship that prevented them from exposing their work to public view, artists developed various strategies of evasion and transgression. Sometimes they tried, with the help of favorable art critics or journalists, to orchestrate press campaigns in which they presented themselves as lucid victims. Courbet was unquestionably one of the cleverest in this regard, as witnesses his correspondence.[70]

Manet sought to mobilize the press over the censorship of his project concerning Maximilian's execution. "I feel that a word about this ridiculously high-handed little act would not be out of place," he wrote in January 1869 to Zola,[71] who a few days later spoke out in *La tribune*: "You can well understand the horror and anger of these censor gentlemen. Just fancy! An artist daring to hold up such a cruel irony before their eyes: France shooting Maximilian!"[72] The effectiveness of such press campaigns depended in the first place on the accuracy with which journalists described works condemned to invisibility, and secondly on the publicity they gave to retributive actions

68. Éric Darragon, *Manet* (Paris: Hachette, 1991), 147ff.

69. Oil on canvas, 1877, Musée de l'Histoire Vivante, Montreuil.

70. ten-Doesschate Chu and Jörg Zutter, *Courbet, artiste et promoteur de son œuvre* (Paris: Flammarion, 1998).

71. Manet to Zola, January 1869, in Françoise Cachin et al., eds., *Manet, 1832–1883: Galeries Nationales du Grand Palais, Paris, April 22-August 8, 1983; Metropolitan Museum of Art, New York, September 10-November 27, 1983* (New York: Harry N. Abrams, 1983), Appendix 2, 529–31.

72. Émile Zola, "Coups d'épingle," *La tribune*, 4 February 1869; reprinted in *Manet, 1832–1883*, 531–32 (translation slightly modified – Tr.).

invariably intended to be discreet and informal, so as to spark controversy and thereby weaken the impact of the censorship.

The only means at artists' disposal to offer some measure of resistance to censorship was to test the limits of the censors' actions by exposing their works via alternative channels. In this respect there were two tools available that sometimes worked in tandem, namely the multiplication of images and private shows. Thus Courbet, Manet, and Pichio proceeded, sometimes clandestinely, to disseminate prints and photographs of censored works. For his *Exécution de Maximilien*, Manet even contemplated distributing a lithograph with the legend purposely erased. But artists' most frequent recourse in the case of prohibitions at the Salon was the parallel public showing. In 1863, for instance, Courbet hung his *Return from the Conference* in his studio. "Everyone is invited," reported Fernand Desnoyers, "to go on any day until noon and look at the picture. People are queuing up."[73] In 1877 Pichio circumvented the censorship of the Republic of Moral Order by showing his *Triomphe de l'ordre* at the gallery of the London Stereoscopic Company, located on Regent Street, where it enjoyed a notable success amplified by a local press well informed by London's network of exiled Communards. In 1885 the painter Maurice Boutet de Monvel sent the Salon jury a monumental canvas entitled *Apothéose de la canaille* (Apotheosis of the Rabble),[74] which was taken as a violently antidemocratic denunciation of the moderate Republic (Figure 5); Edmond Turquet, sometime State Undersecretary of Fine Arts, thought he recognized himself in one of the bloated faces of the populace in the foreground. Accepted at first, the work was taken down a few days prior to the show's official opening on the grounds that it was liable to "provoke dangerous or disagreeable altercation in the midst of the Salon."[75] The newspaper *Le Figaro*, which had criticized this decision, immediately welcomed the censored picture, hanging it on the back wall of the great subscription hall on the ground floor of its premises on Rue Drouot, where the general public could come and see it.[76] Meanwhile *L'illustration* guaranteed the work wide exposure by reproducing it on its front page.[77]

73. Fernand Desnoyers, *Salon des Refusés: La peinture en 1863* (Paris: Dutil, 1863).
74. Oil on canvas, 1884, Musée des Beaux-Arts, Orléans.
75. J. V., "Nouvel incident au Salon," *Le Figaro*, 22 April 1885.
76. "Exposition du tableau de M. Boutet de Monvel au *Figaro*," *Le Figaro*, 8 May 1885.
77. *L'illustration*, 25 April 1885, 300.

Figure 5. Maurice Boutet de Monvel, *Apothéose de la canaille*, also known as *Le triomphe de Robert Macaire*, oil on canvas, 1884. Musée des beaux-arts, Orléans.

The backdrop to the retributive measures taken by political régimes against works that they wanted to hide from view, as likewise to the strategies adopted by artists to circumvent such censoring, was the fear of the power of the work of art—regardless of its aesthetic merits—as a dangerous image. Governments, authoritarian and liberal alike, also feared the dangerous capacity of the distribution and public exhibition of images liable to inflame passions and proliferate. As a journalist put it apropos of Pichio's *Triomphe de l'ordre*:

> What are we to think of the impression made by prints that portray the agents of riot and crime as martyrs or sympathetic heroes? To produce works with such intentions is a reprehensible act; and a danger, an incitement to criminal folly, and wherever they are found works of this nature should be swept away, eliminated, for the sake of morality and public order.[78]

—Translated by Donald Nicholson-Smith

78. "L'excitation à l'émeute," *La patrie*, 5 April 1875.

DONALD E. ENGLISH

Anxiety and the Official Censorship of the Photographic Image, 1850–1900

Within twenty years of its discovery in 1839 by Louis Daguerre, photography was widely popular throughout France. Rarely does a technical invention capture the imagination of an era so quickly, and integrate itself into a culture and people's everyday lives with such ease. It is therefore not surprising that, as with the other visual arts in the nineteenth century, this influential new medium was used for political purposes. So great was the concern and even fear among authorities over its potential power that control of the production, distribution, and circulation of photographs was a serious issue for officials throughout the 1850–1900 period. It would subside only when the vast number of images published in the popular press at the end of the century made it simply impossible to manage. Until then, political censorship of the photographic image was the rule rather than the exception.

Early in the Second Empire photography emerged as a significant economic and cultural phenomenon and most people in France initially encountered it through commercial photography. From 1848 to 1871 this new industry grew steadily as the number of businesses specializing in portraiture expanded under Napoleon III. For example, in the late 1860s, 365 photographic studios were listed in the commercial directories for Paris alone. By the end of the century that number had grown to nearly 1,400 professional photographers in the capital and approximately 2,000 others in the provinces.[1] In the 1880s

1. *Résultats statistiques de recensements des industries et professions. Dénombrement général de la population du 1896. Région de Paris au Nord de l'Est, I* (Paris: Imprimerie nationale, 1899), 242. *Résultats statistiques de recensements des industries et professions. Dénombrement général de la population de 1896. Résultats généraux, IV* (Paris: Imprimerie nationale, 1901), 214. See also an excellent study by

YFS 122, *Out of Sight: Political Censorship of the Visual Arts in Nineteenth-Century France,* ed. Goldstein, © 2012 by Yale University.

a series of technical and scientific breakthroughs led to the gradual evolution of smaller, lighter, portable, hand-held cameras that formed an instantaneous image on light sensitive film, rather than on a bulky glass plate. Working professionals were now joined by thousands of amateur photographers who made literally hundreds of thousands of pictures each year, which were often sold or traded among friends. Paralleling this general expansion was the introduction of photography into magazines and newspapers at the end of the century, which was facilitated by the technical development of the half-tone printing process. Just as this invention revolutionized journalism, it also made possible the mass production of photographs on posters, leaflets, brochures, and books. Thereafter, inexpensive pictures appeared practically everywhere in a variety of formats as millions of images circulated throughout the country, and photography became generally accepted as the standard form of visual communication in almost all printed materials.[2]

Portraiture was initially the most common application of photography since the inability of early cameras to record movement simply made stationary objects more suitable. But the popularity of carte-de-visite photographs beginning in the 1850s also contributed to the dominance of the portrait to the visual history of this era. These small images were at first the domain of notables in France, but they soon gained acceptance among the emerging middle classes as well, who sought to emulate the appearances of their social superiors by sitting for the cartes themselves, and then eventually purchasing images of well known aristocrats, politicians, artists, and intellectuals for their personal home collections. As with other visual arts, these photographs were considered both a mirror and a window into the individuality of the sitter. Accordingly, representation of people in such portraits was viewed as a sign of their inner qualities—no less

---

Elizabeth Anne McCauley, *Industrial Madness: Commercial Photography in Paris, 1848–1871* (New Haven: Yale University Press, 1994), passim.

2. The first photo interview in a French newspaper was published in 1886 by *Le journal* when the well-known photographer Nadar interviewed the noted scientist Eugène Chevreul on the occasion of his one hundredth birthday. The illustrated weekly news and general interest magazine *L'illustration* published its first photograph in 1891. On the integration of photomechanical processes into magazine and newspaper production, see Claude Bellanger, Jacques Godeschot, Pierre Guiral, and Fernand Terrou, eds. *Histoire générale de la press française* (Paris: Presses universitaires de France, 1972), v. III, 95–97, 122–23, 280, 387; and Eugène Courmont, *Histoire et technique de la photogravure* (Paris: Gauthier-Villars, 1947), passim.

than their internal moral character and genetic potential as individuals. Thus, the face of the subject was believed to be penetrated by the lens to reveal his personality and temperament, while the outward pose, dress, and studio props in the portrait showed his class and profession. This portrait photograph was considered more truthful and objective than the subjective, hand-composed illustration of an artist because what appeared in the photographic image was actually and literally the physical manifestation of an authentic person at a unique moment in time. In perfect harmony with the dominant intellectual current of the time, Positivism, this new medium was so closely associated with the contemporary discourse of scientific knowledge and truth that the photograph was assumed then (and still is by many today) to be an unmediated copy of "reality."[3]

How photographs work as communication, of course, is far more complex. Just as people are born into a society that has a pre-established language, and approach the world through it, so too they confront a ready-made visual field that they must learn to comprehend. This visual field is composed of a variety of codes and symbols that have developed over time in the society and culture. Photographs thus communicate within an interpretive context in which the historical traditions of an era, and its social, political, and economic structures situate their meaning for both their producers and viewers. They provide powerful and potentially persuasive information about the people, places, and events that they represent.[4]

---

3. On the social and psychological significance of the carte-de-visite photograph, see McCauley, *A.A.E. Disderi and the Carte-de-Visite Portrait Photograph* (New Haven: Yale University Press, 1985), passim.; and G. Rongier, "Du portrait artistique," *L'amateur photographie* (May 1, 1888): 223–27.

4. Scholarship on the polysemic function of photography as communication and modern visual culture encompasses several disciplines, theories, and methodologies. Among others, see Pierre Bourdieu, *Un art moyen, essai sur les usages de la photographie* (Paris: Les Éditions de Minuit, 1965); Roland Barthes, *Camera Lucida*, trans. Richard Howard (New York: Hill and Wang, 1981); Victor Burgin, *Thinking Photography* (London: Macmillan, 1983); John Tagg, *The Burden of Representation: Essays on Photographies and Histories* (Amherst: University of Massachusetts Press, 1988); Peter Burke, *Eyewitnessing: The Uses of Images as Historical Evidence* (Ithaca, NY: Cornell University Press, 2001); Theo Van Leeuwen and Carey Jewitt, eds., *Handbook of Visual Analysis* (London: Sage, 2001); Gilian Rose, ed., *Visual Methodologies: An Introduction to the Interpretation of Visual Materials* (London: Sage, 2001); Ken Smith, ed., *Handbook of Visual Communication: Theory, Methods, and Media* (Mahwah, New Jersey: Erlbaum, 2005); and Jessica Evans and Stuart Hall, eds., *Visual Culture: The Reader* (London: Sage, 1999).

The first legal restrictions on the photographic image came with Napoleon III's Decree of February 17, 1852. Extending the censorship laws of 1835, it was designed to regulate all printed matter and images, including those photographs exhibited, sold, or distributed to the public. Henceforth such pictures were required to receive authorization from the Ministry of the Interior or departmental prefects, and copies of each were to be deposited in a copyright registry, including on each the name and address of the photographer and printer. By the 1860s over 9,000 photographs were already registered in this official archive, while those that did not receive authorization were subject to confiscation and the photographers to fines. In effect, the registry functioned as the initial method for state censorship by controlling the number of images that could circulate throughout the country and restricting their places of registration. That anxiety at the highest level of the government underlay these early restrictions was apparent in court cases that would soon follow. For example, one case filed in the Imperial Court at Aix in 1859 prompted the Ministers of the Interior and Justice to resurrect an old 1814 law regulating the press, and then apply it to the current commercial uses of photography. The specific circumstances involved a photographer named Nadal who had reproduced and sold photographs that he did not originally take. In their discussion about the possible illegality and the nuisance of copyright infringement, the ministers expressed even more concern with the potential power of the new medium to "put itself in the service of evil passions which society could not protect against." They raised the issue with the Emperor himself, and all three were convinced that future censorship would both protect the public and provide the means for government surveillance of a new influential medium without unduly sacrificing its future growth as an economic industry.[5]

The second method of controlling the photographic image involved an individual's right to the visual representation of himself as private property. This was especially salient due to the immense popularity of carte-de-visite portraits in the Second Empire, and the lucrative business of selling celebrity pictures. And by the late 1850s court cases establishing the parameters of this right began to appear.

5. Archives nationales de France (hereafter cited at AN). Series BB, Ministère de la Justice. BB18, 1626/4342, "Consulte du Ministère de l'Intérieur sur un projet de soumettre la photographie à la loi du 21 Octobre 1814," March 13, 1861. Here and throughout, translations are my own unless noted otherwise.

Perhaps the most noted was brought in 1867 by the well known author Alexander Dumas against a photographer named Alphonse Liébert. This lensman had sold portraits of Dumas, asserting that since the author did not originally pay for the pictures he had the right to sell them as his own. Dumas objected and the court eventually ruled in his favor, while other rulings then held that even after the sitter's death the family, not the photographer, controlled the right to the deceased's image.[6]

Outright censorship of photographs during the Second Empire was limited to three general areas of illicit imagery. Among these were photographs considered an outrage to "bonnes moeurs," that is, principally obscene pictures of nude women or men and women grouped in indecent sexual positions. Still others were considered an outrage to the "morale publique et réligieuse" and usually represented priests, monks, and prelates in lubricious poses or committing acts of immorality. The third category, politically seditious photographs, almost all represented the sovereign Napoleon III or his family in insulting, scandalous, or shameful poses. From 1858 to 1881, 68 individuals were arrested for distribution of these prohibited images, the highest number in 1864 when 33 were incarcerated. But as the press laws were liberalized in the late 1860s, the number of prosecutions declined markedly.[7]

The Paris Commune of 1871 provided the occasion for the camera to play an important new role. There was no full-time, official photographer assigned to capture the momentous events of the upheaval, but several remained in Paris during the siege and took pictures of the barricades and the men and women who defended them. No pictures exist of the actual fighting due to the inherent danger involved in setting up the bulky equipment. But after the government's final

6. On the legal aspects of French photography, see Édouard Sauvel, *Études de droit sur la photographie* (Paris: Charles Mendel: n.d.), and his *De la propriété artistique de photographie* (Paris: Gauthier-Villars, 1897); E.N. Santini, *La photographie devant les tribunaux* (Paris: Charles Mendel: n.d.); Armand Bigeon, *La photographie devant la loi et devant la jurisprudence* (Paris: Société d'éditions scientifiques: 1892); and McCauley, "Merely Mechanical: On the Origins of Photographic Copyright in France and Great Britain," *Art History* (February 2008): 57–78.

7. Fernand Drujon, *Catalogue des ouvrages, écrits, et dessins de toute nature poursuivis, supprimés ou condamnés, 1814–1877* (Paris: Édouard Rouveyre: 1879) XXIX-XXX. On the censorship of pornographic photographs, see David Ogawa, "Arresting Nudes in the Second Empire," *History of Photography* (Winter 2007): 330–47; and Susan Waller, "Censors and Photographs in the Third Republic," *History of Photography* (Autumn 2003): 222–36.

victory in the spring of 1871, cameramen returned to take pictures
of the destruction, including thousands of corpses in the temporary
morgues in the city and at Versailles. The deadly conflict and the ruin
of so many historic buildings had generated a huge market for pictures of the desolation not only across France, but also in the rest of
Europe. To those who could not travel to Paris and see for themselves,
the photographs were at once eyewitness accounts and souvenirs of
the tragedy. Commercial cameramen, of course, were especially interested in making money and quickly sought to fulfill the public
demand for visual reproductions. As early as July, for example, the
well known photographer Disderi had completed a portrait collection
of Communard leaders and a series representing the ruins, which he
made available for sale in bookstores and photograph shops throughout the country. Over 50,000 images of the toppled Vendôme Column
were sent to London within weeks of the original event to satisfy
British curiosity.[8]

Many of these images were soon collected and sold in albums
and books accompanied by captions that gave unique political significance to the events. The words, of course, shaped the meaning of
the pictures by directing the viewers' interpretation, and those that
appeared in the immediate aftermath were almost all unfavorable to
the Communards. Only later in the century, when adverse public reaction had waned, did these captioned images become more benign.
Among the most provocative of these was a series of composite photographs entitled "Crimes of the Commune" by the Parisian photographer Eugène Appert. These nine images combined actual photographs
and hand compositions into scenes of historical events primarily emphasizing the gruesome execution of hostages and the administration
of justice to Communard officials. Appert had received permission
from the government to photograph various prisoners at Versailles
who were involved in these events. He then placed their portraits
on the bodies of models who posed for the compositions. The quality of the images varied from sophisticated to obviously fabricated,
but given the public knowledge of photomontage techniques at the
time, few questioned the accuracy or authenticity of the pictures,
considering them to be faithful representations of the real events. An
examination of two images reveals the differences. In the Execution

8. In advertisement, *Le charivari*, (July 2, 1871): 4; and Jules Moinaux, "Revue
comique des tribunaux," *Le charivari* (July 3, 1871): 2–3.

of Generals Clément-Thomas and Lecomte (Figure 1), the figures in the scene may appear stiff and unnatural to a critical viewer today, but only under a magnifying glass can the combined photographs and the retouched background be discerned. On the other hand, the representation of the Massacre of Argueil Dominicans (Figure 2) appears highly contrived and unnatural, as the edges delineating the overlapping photographs are clearly visible to the naked eye.[9]

While Appert was making these highly polemical composite images, he and other photographers also began to sell portrait photographs of Communard leaders and pictures of the city's ruins. In the early weeks after the conflict, literally thousands of these circulated individually or in collections. One of the immediate tasks of Parisian authorities was then to reassert control over their unrestricted flow. At the end of June they revived the old law of April 17, 1852, which required that all images, including photographs, be authorized by the Ministry of the Interior. Enforcement was initially difficult due to the vast number of pictures still in circulation and the immense profit potential in their sale. The illicit trade was well worth the risk of heavy fines and prison sentences for many photographers and businessmen.[10] The Ministry then followed up this renewed policy in Paris with an ordinance on sales nationwide. It especially focused on prior authorization for street vendors, hawkers, and travelling peddlers who were instrumental in establishing an informal but effective distribution network across the country. Concerned these itinerant vendors might spread potentially dangerous materials, the Minister called for special enforcement against them beyond the original regulations. In his private instructions to local officials, he mandated individualized physical searches of all packs, boxes, and wagons of these peddlers.[11] Many photographers, on the other hand, including Appert and a well known cameraman named Pierre Petit, had duly registered their images and received permission to sell them freely. Their names and addresses were kept by the authorities who knew where to locate them if different restrictions on circulation were necessary. But others did not comply, and the number of both legal and illicit photographs swelled in the following months. Public interest in them was

9. Donald E. English, "Political Photography and the Paris Commune of 1871: The Photographs of Eugène Appert," *History of Photography* (Winter 2003): 31–42.

10. Archives de la Préfecture de Police, Paris (hereafter cited as APP), BA/365–4, Commune de Paris, October 23 and 31, 1871.

11. APP, BA/1621, Presse et Censure, October 15, 1871.

Figure 1. Eugène Appert. Execution of Generals Clémont-Thomas and Lecomte. 1871. Bibliothèque nationale (BnF).

CRIMES DE LA COMMUNE

VICTIMES

T. R. P. Captier
R. P. Bourard
R. P. Delhorme
R. P. Cotrault
R. P. Chatagneret
R. P. Guillemet
Gauquelin (Louis)
Volano (François)
Gros (Aimé)
Marc (Antoine)
Cathala (Théodore)
Dintroz (Françoise)
Cabanial (Joseph)
Petit (Germain)

ÉCHAPPÉS AU MASSACRE

L'abbé Grancolas (Joseph)
Bertrand (Édouard)
Rigollot (Jean-Baptiste)
Gauvain (Édouard)
Delassus (Prosper)
Ducré (Antoine)
Broume (Simon)

FÉDÉRÉS

Léo Meillet, membre de la Commune
Lucipia, procureur de la Commune
Sérizier, colonel du 101e
Boin, capitaine au 101e
Beaupois, lieutenant au 101e
Rouillac, lieutenant au 101e
Thaler, gouverneur du fort de Bicêtre
Boudalix, lieutenant du 101e
Pascal, lieutenant au 177e
Quesnot, commandant du 120e
Gibsoch, lieutenant au 120e
Graspe, fédéré au 176e
Frasse, fédéré au 101e
Bosquart, lieutenant au 102e
Gambette, tambour au 101e
Buppo, fédéré au 101e
Abat, fédéré au 101e

MASSACRE DES DOMINICAINS D'ARCUEIL
Route d'Italie, N° 38, le 25 Mai 1871, à 4 heures et demie.

Figure 2. Eugène Appert. Massacre of Argueil Dominicans. 1871. BnF.

intense. One journalist explained how the portrait photographs of the Communard leaders especially seemed to provide special insight into the soul of these men at a time when curiosity was superseded by a deep-seated need to comprehend the unprecedented acts of cruelty and destruction that had occurred during the fighting.[12]

These pictures and their immense popularity deeply troubled government officials who feared their potentially unsettling effects on the public. At the end of December 1871, using the power given to him under the state of siege that still officially prevailed in Paris, the Military Governor of Paris banned all photographs that were said to "disturb the public peace." Those scenes depicting actions by the Commune, its defenders, committee meetings or demonstrations by the Commune government, and all images of the repression by Versailles were censored. Especially forbidden were portraits of individuals under prosecution or convicted for participation in the insurrection. On November 25, 1872, similar orders went out to police in all departments, establishing nationwide prohibition of most photographs related to the Commune. Only those pictures that were deemed purely artistic images of the ruins and fires in Paris escaped censorship. Even Appert, who had initially received permission to sell his representations, was impacted, as all previous authorizations were now reversed.[13]

Several months of vigilant enforcement were necessary to get these pictures off the streets. The dealers were so scattered and they operated in such unusual ways that implementation of the ban was always difficult. For example, Appert's series "Crimes of the Commune" had been inserted inside tapioca boxes sold wholesale to local grocers as part of an advertising campaign to attract customers. The police often had to rely upon informers in order to locate and intercept the pictures, and dutifully followed up all leads for the next three years.[14] It may seem today paradoxical for the government to censor photographs that supported the official position about the insurrection, but it testifies to the power of these pictures to elicit popular emotions about the fighting that the authorities felt were best forgotten. They felt that one way to veil those memories and to reduce the chances of the recurrence of such violence was to ban all images,

12. Ernest Legouvé, "Un album photographique," *Le petit journal* (October 27, 1871): 2.
13. "Chronique", *Gazette des tribunaux* (December 31, 1871): 911.
14. AN, BB 24, 793, Demandes des Grâces, Dossier 5606.

regardless of whether they supported the government's role in the events.

Overt censorship of a particular political opponent's photographic materials awaited the resurgence of the Bonapartist movement in the mid 1870s. Technically, photographs of the Imperial family had been banned since 1872 by the same decree that outlawed photographs of the Commune. This original prohibition included all portraits in which members of the Bonapartist family wore Imperial emblems or scenes where they performed acts that depicted or implied their political sovereignty in France. Simple portraits of the family dressed in civilian clothes were not illegal if they did not include their former titles.[15] However, given the deluge of images related to the Parisian insurrection, the authorities did not strictly enforce the ordinance in the immediately ensuing years. All that changed with the surprising strength shown by Bonapartist candidates in thirteen by-elections held between May, 1874 and February, 1875 when they won five seats and compiled impressive vote totals in five others. The election of a Bonapartist in the Department of the Nièvre over a more heavily favored Republican candidate especially frightened government officials who soon after opened both judicial and legislative investigations into Bonapartist political activities. What they found was an elaborate organization headquartered in Paris with grass roots local committees throughout the provinces, and a sophisticated propaganda arm that found great political value in the distribution of photographs to rural voters. Léon Renault, Prefect of Police in Paris, contributed to both reports and emphasized the importance of this photographic propaganda, concluding that it was a serious threat. "I repeat, the effect of these images is considerable, and the committee members have been so convinced, that they have spared nothing in order to develop this propaganda which is . . . more effective in awakening and perpetuating the memories of the Empire." As early as 1873 the central committee had ordered two large printings of over 400,000 portraits of the Bonapartist heir, the Prince Imperial, and it had plans to distribute seven million more prior to the general elections of 1875. These portraits were, of course, vulnerable to the official sanction, but the Bonapartists had eluded confiscation by sending them through the mail to addresses provided both by public officials

---

15. *Recueil officiel des circulaires émanées de la Préfecture de Police, 1849–1880* (Paris: Imprimerie Chaix, 1883), 290.

who still supported their cause and by political sympathizers who donated their guest lists for various celebrations. Although the police had been carefully observing the materials of street vendors and peddlers, the Bonapartists avoided these channels of distribution altogether, and instead had their supporters present the pictures informally to people they met during the course of the day.[16]

Faced with this significant electoral challenge, the government's response was both deep and wide. Surveillance, arrests, prosecutions, fines, and prison sentences for the illegal sale or free distribution of Imperial portraits mounted throughout the summer and fall of 1874. Among the censored images was "Principle of National Sovereignty and the Flag that It Consecrates" (Figure 3). In this composite photograph, the Prince Imperial, wearing civilian clothes, holds a tricolor flag and points to an urn with the slogan "universal suffrage," as if to suggest his overall acceptance of the Republic and democracy. Yet at the top of the flag pole resides the Imperial eagle, and the national sovereignty appears to be entrusted to one man, the heir to the Napoleonic dynasty. Back in Paris, Eugène Appert was arrested and fined for an unauthorized composite portrait he made of the Prince Imperial. The police then moved to eliminate the photographs at their source. The administrators of the Bonapartist photographic propaganda, a merchant named Henri Guérard and a photographer named Valentin, were both arrested and fined for the production and sale of the banned images. More importantly, the authorities confiscated and destroyed several hundred thousand photographs before these two men could send them into the provinces. The case against a retired rural policeman named Desbois in the Department of Nièvre also revealed the extent to which the authorities would go in stopping the flow of these photographs, and the importance they attributed to them. Locally known and respected, Desbois was an old-line Bonapartist who walked the back roads and visited small villages outside Nevers, distributing portrait photographs of the Prince Imperial to whomever he met, and requesting from these residents their vote in return. In their investigation the police located every individual to whom Desbois had talked, confiscated their photographs, and interrogated them about how many pictures he carried, how many he gave away, where he got the pictures, and whom else he met. They concluded

16. *Annales de l'Assemblée nationale, Compte-rendus in extenso des séances. Annexes. Tome XXXVII* (March 1–20, 1875): 277; *Tome XL 13–30* (July 1875): 115.

Figure 3. Principle of National Sovereignty and the Flag that Consecrates It. 1874. BnF.

that personalized dissemination of the photographs was both favorably received and influential in affecting the voters' preferences in the local elections.[17]

17. *Annales, Tome XXXVII*, (March 1–20, 1875): 361–370; "Chroniques", *Gazette des tribunaux* (July 15, 1874): 672; "Tribunal correctionnel de Paris, Portraits pho-

In January 1875, the Court of Cassation in Paris eliminated an important loophole in the law that required prior authorization for these photographs. Strictly interpreted, this regulation applied to merchants, business people, and photographers who sold, displayed, or gave away images but not necessarily to private individuals. Many of the Bonapartist distributors of these pictures claimed they did not come under this rule, as they were simply exchanging the photographs with friends and neighbors. The court concluded, however, that all individuals who disseminated the photographs in any way were responsible under the law. Thereafter authorization for all photographs sent through the mail to political supporters, or just given away to friends was also compulsory.[18] In February 1875, Cornelius de Witt, undersecretary of the Ministry of Interior, followed up with re-enforced censorship on all photographs of the Imperial heir, withdrawing any previous authorization for portraits of the Prince regardless of whether they were simple images of him in civilian clothes without Imperial insignia. De Witt concluded that these photographs were no less political propaganda than the illegal portraits, having the same intention and affect as the others, and that they should therefore be included in the official censorship. Furthermore, sorting out the thousands of authorized and unauthorized images in circulation at the same time had become too difficult and confusing for the police, and in the next two years most of the Bonapartist photographs in circulation were eliminated.[19]

Only in 1879 did the Bonapartists again mount a significant attempt to renew their political influence. The fortunes of the movement had ebbed in the intervening years with the death of Napoleon III. The Imperial heir now tried to reinvigorate the party and his popularity by joining the British army and volunteering for service in colonial Africa. Reestablishing political relevance through heroic efforts in battle, as his great uncle had done earlier in the century, might have succeeded, but the young Prince Imperial was unexpectedly killed in combat with Zulu warriors on June 1, 1879. The event, however, did provide the occasion for his supporters back in France to take advantage of the tragedy with the last massive distribution

tographiques du Prince Imperial non-autorisés," *Gazette des tribunaux* (September 11, 1874): 872.

18. "Cour de Cassation. Distribution des photographies," *Gazette des tribunaux* (January 2–3, 1875): 5.

19. APP, BA/419, Affaires bonapartistes, March 8, 1875.

of photographs by the Bonapartists in the nineteenth century. Soon thereafter various images of the young Prince began circulating in France, especially at the functions where supporters were gathering to mourn the loss of their leader. Fearing the effects of the images on the attendees, the government's crackdown was again swift, especially in Paris where thousands had been attending the numerous memorial masses. All the images were clearly illegal by previous ordinances since they represented the Bonapartist heir in imperial regalia or were funeral cards that also included portraits of other Bonapartist notables who still lived in France. One image (Figure 4) was more elaborate, a skillful photomontage depicting the actual scene of the Prince's death in the African bush at the hands of the Zulu tribesmen. This image might have been an effective political tool since it more truly imparted the Napoleonic myth of heroic activity in the service of individual and national honor, but it too was banned and confiscated wherever it appeared.[20] Overall, the Bonapartists were the first political movement in France to recognize the effectiveness of photographs, and to use them systematically to influence voters. Their activities in the mid 1870s paid off initially in numerous electoral victories where their old loyalists still remained. But the government's censorship after those early victories was a significant blow, and by the end of the decade the party's fortunes had declined. The lesson for those in power was that vigilant censorship of photographic propaganda could counter the political influence of an opponent, and that in time of challenge or crisis it was an invaluable tool for the preservation of the existing regime.

The establishment of more liberal press laws in 1881 reflected growing confidence in the strength and legitimacy of Republican institutions by officials. Under these new regulations the onerous restrictions requiring prior authorization of photographs, as well as other visual materials, were lifted. Professional photographers, however, were nevertheless still required to identify clearly their names and addresses on their products. Anxieties about the image lingered, even if overall efforts at surveillance and censorship diminished over the next few years, as always in the background was the anticipation of a new political crisis. It came with the unexpected and meteoric rise of General Georges Boulanger and his quest, in conjunction with other

20. AN, BB30, 1123, Colportages et Élections, June 24, 1879; APP, BA/1203, Mort du Prince Imperial, June 26-September 30, 1879.

Figure 4. Death of the Prince Imperial. 1879. BnF.

conservatives, to end the Republic in the late 1880s. Impressed by recent American innovations in political campaigns, Boulanger and the monarchist heir to the throne sought to influence French voters through massive propaganda distributions that foretold truly modern publicity techniques. In doing so they extensively utilized photography and other visual materials, along with posters, leaflets, songs, and brochures. Early electoral successes again worried Republican officials, who were now faced with abrogating the newly established press freedoms in order to curtail the growing popularity and potential danger of Boulanger and the royalists. The General, in particular, found portrait photographs to be among his most effective tools, distributing literally millions of these pictures during the by-elections of 1888. Some of the images were produced outside of France in either Belgium or Germany, and did not include the name and address of the photographer. Thus the police were well within the law to confiscate them as they appeared in the northern departments where Boulanger was especially popular.[21]

Royalist photographic propaganda was more limited, often interspersed with other lithographic images depicting the royalist pretender, the Comte de Paris, who had been exiled from France earlier in 1886. Such was concern over all these pictures circulating in this heated electoral environment that the Ministry of the Interior finally sent out orders to police across France to confiscate five images of Boulanger and the Comte. Additional plans were developed to censor another fourteen pictures.[22] Even though portrait photographs were not among the original photos banned, they were, not surprisingly, caught up in the purge of the other images. Inquiries soon streamed back to departmental prefects and to the Ministry from local officials who sought clarification on what could or could not be seized. In the Department of Calvados, the prefect's response was typical: as if anticipating the confusion, he simply ordered the seizure of all photographs. Then after the local police had cleared the streets of the pictures he would sort out later what specifically could be banned.[23]

21. AN, F7, 12448, Agissements boulangistes, July 7, October 18, October 24, October 26, 1888.
22. AN, F7, 12928, Saisie des déssins, October 27, 1888; F7, 12853, Propagande royaliste, October 30, 1888.
23. AN, F7, 12928, Lettre de la Préfecture du Calvados au Ministère de l'Intérieur, December 11, 1888.

Such aggressive censorship immediately generated a response, and legal suits challenging the confiscation of these pictures were filed in the Departments of Loiret, Calvados, Morbihan, Lot-et-Garonne, Charentes Inférior, Orne, and the Indre-et-Loire in the late autumn of 1888. In all these cases the government's defense was similar, providing an instructive look at the justification for censorship in the new era of press freedom. Attorneys emphasized the seditious and evil purposes of the images, arguing that they were treasonous and designed to upset the public order. In addition, they argued that the seizures were administrative acts of the Ministry of the Interior and, given the legal separation between the judicial and administrative functions of the state going back to the eighteenth century, the courts had no jurisdiction. Moreover, they maintained, in time of crisis, even under the new press laws, the government could perform actions in the interests of national security for which it could not be held accountable by the courts. And finally, officials were only carrying out the intent of the Law of Exile of 1886, which had banned the monarchist pretender from France and so, too, his visual propaganda. Decisions in these cases began to appear in the winter and spring of 1889, and all went against the government. The courts ruled that by their very nature these confiscations were police actions and not administrative acts. And even if the Ministry of the Interior censored in the name of national security, the law referred only to periods of crisis such as a time of war or siege. Since France was definitely not in such a crisis, extraordinary censorship to protect the security of the nation at that time was held illegal, a clear violation of the press law of 1881. Even if the law exiling the royalist pretender banned his person from France it did not explicitly prohibit his visual materials. Soon after these decisions, the Ministry of the Interior withdrew its directives and instructed all prefects on March 30, 1889, to return the confiscated materials to the various political groups.[24]

In the meantime, before the final resolution of these cases, General Boulanger had mounted the most extensive visual publicity campaign in the history of France. He successfully got his image before the voters, and showed impressive electoral strength in seven northern departments, culminating in a lopsided victory in the Paris by-election of January 1889. Fearing the consequences of imminent

24. "Tribunal de conflits," *Gazette des tribunaux* (March 27, 1889): 297.

electoral defeat, the government finally took new measures to stop his momentum. On March 2, 1889, the Minister of the Interior ordered the seizure of all Boulangist propaganda, especially the portrait photographs of the general that had been received with such widespread enthusiasm by French voters (Figure 5).[25] Despite the legal clarifications that emerged in late March, in the following weeks and months this censorship expanded. Millions of photographs were eventually confiscated and destroyed, even after Boulanger fled to Belgium to avoid the charge of plotting to overthrow the nation.[26] Overall, the authorities during these critical months wielded the state's power in deliberate disregard of the prevailing press laws, gambling that its open and blatant action would not generate greater sympathy for their opponents. When these efforts proved successful, as in earlier times, it set a powerful precedent. Illegal censorship had clearly worked to remove visual materials from view, and by the time a political rival could seek redress through the judicial system the political crisis had passed and the Republic had been spared.

The Dreyfus Affair, however, proved a more serious challenge. While Boulanger's threat to the status quo was problematic, it was still fought through the ballot box. By the late 1890s the nationalist, royalist, and anti-Semitic groups that formed the backbone of the anti-Dreyfusard movement had rejected electoral politics altogether and were advocating the elimination of the Third Republic by whatever means possible. Moreover, loyalty of both the army, given the nature of the controversy, and vast portions of the population especially in conservative western France where Dreyfus was standing trial, were in question. Emboldened by these possibilities, these rightist groups sought to agitate the populace and channel emotional discontent into support for revolution or a coup d'état. The monarchists especially, led now by the young heir Duc d'Orléans, and the extremist nationalist party, the Ligue des Patriotes headed by Paul Déroulède, were the most aggressive. They initiated a propaganda campaign that coupled visual materials with an attempt to elicit military and popular support for a march on Paris in the summer of 1899. Rumors were rife about the potential coup, and the Republican authorities stepped in, arrested the leaders of these groups, and confiscated several hundred

25. APP, BA/971, Propagande boulangiste, March 3, 1889.
26. AN, F7, 12448, Agissements boulangistes, May 11, 1889; APP, BA/971, Propagande boulangiste, June 29, July 24–25, August 8, 1889.

Figure 5. Bengue. General Georges Boulanger. 1888. BnF.

thousand photographs before their distribution in western France. Among these was the poster "Dreyfus Is a Traitor" (Figure 6). Produced by the Ligue des Patriotes, it presents the portraits of five former Ministers of War who had resigned in protest over the government's handling of the Dreyfus Affair. In the fall of 1899 the rightist leaders stood trial for conspiracy to overthrow the Republic. Evidence in the proceedings included crate after crate of this photographic propaganda. For the first time photographs were used as physical evidence in a case documenting a dramatic attempt to overthrow the government and were vivid testament to the assumed power that these images would have on the behavior of vulnerable viewers.[27]

Just as important as these large-scale distributions of individual photographs for political purposes were new developments in photographic technology that were taking the medium in a new and eventually more influential direction. In the 1890s, highly light sensitive photographic emulsions, roll film, and portable cameras vastly expanded the appropriate subject matter for the photographer by making it possible to capture transitory political events. With this new technology also came the introduction of photographs into magazines and newspapers, creating a new profession and method of visual communication—photojournalism.[28] Leaders of conservative groups, especially, recognized that photographs of their activities that were reproduced in nationally distributed publications could give more enduring life and wider dissemination to their activities than ever before. They also learned early on that these new photographers and reporters could be exploited with "media events" designed to manipulate the coverage of the burgeoning modern press. In this journalistic environment, official censorship had to take a new direction if it were to be effective in controlling the visual information of political opponents.

Such censorship took the form of restrictions on photographers' access to controversial political events, thereby regulating the type of images that could be captured for later publication. Among the

27. *Haute Cour de Justice: Affaire Buffet, Déroulède, Guérin, et autres inculpés de complot* (Paris: Imprimerie nationale, 1899). *Documents. Renseignements généraux,* 18, 29; *Documents. Group royaliste,* 29–30, 43–44, 74–75; *Documents. Ligue des Patriotes,* 29; APP, BA/1034, Paul Déroulède, October 6, 1899.

28. The first photo interview of a political figure in France was that of General Georges Boulanger. See Charles Chincholle, "Entrevue photographique," *Le Figaro. Supplément littéraire* (November 23, 1889).

Figure 6. E. Charaire. Dreyfus is a Traitor. 1898. Archives nationales (F7, 12463).

prohibitions was the trial of Captain Dreyfus in Rennes during the summer of 1899. Employees of the photo-illustrated magazines, of course, objected, arguing that while they were excluded other artists, etchers, and even caricaturists, who often made a mockery of the participants and the court, were allowed to attend. One photojournalist from the popular *L'illustration*, Edmond Frank, even hypothesized that beyond the fear of the new was a more significant anxiety over the inner revelation that could come from a photograph. He observed, "Such is its power that it holds under its yoke even men of high intelligence and culture . . . the camera seems to frighten these men as a diabolical instrument which, while recording their images, consumes their intimate personality and steals part of their soul."[29] The camera apparently would turn the people and proceedings into an even more significant phenomenon than officials wanted. Thus, all photographers were banned. The pictures of the courtroom that do exist and that eventually made it into the press were unauthorized, secretly snapped by hidden cameras and are of poor quality, taken from distant or uninformative visual angles (Figure 7).[30]

Censorship of those opponents who sought to exploit the photopress for their own political purposes took a similar direction. For example, the most creative and aggressive visual propagandist at the end of the century was Jules Guérin, head of the right-wing Ligue Antisémitique. In an effort to spread his virulent message against Jews he became a master at innovative techniques, including the publication of an early photo-illustrated newspaper *L'antijuif illustré*. Guérin and his followers participated with other conservatives in the conspiracy to overthrow the government during the summer of the Dreyfus trial in Rennes. When Paris police armed with an arrest warrant arrived at his headquarters on the Rue Chabrol in the tenth arrondisement on August 14, 1899, he and several associates barricaded the entrance and refused to surrender. In what became known as the "Fort Chabrol Affair," police agents laid siege to the building for six weeks. By the second week press coverage made Guérin, his political viewpoints, and his resistance to the government known to the entire country. The photograph-illustrated news magazines, including *La vie*

29. Edmond Frank, "Pour le photographe," *L'illustration* (November 12, 1898): 307.

30. AN, F7, 12464, Affaire Dreyfus, July 4, 1899. Many scenes that do exist of the trial and its environs appeared in the illustrated weekly journals during the summer and fall of 1899 including *Le monde illustré*, *La vie illustrée*, *L'illustration*, *L'univers illustré*, and *L'instantané*.

PENDANT L'AUDIENCE DU CONSEIL DE GUERRE

Figure 7. M. Gribayéoff. During the Audience of the Council of War. August 12, 1899. *L'univers illustré*. BnF.

illustrée, Le monde illustré, L'univers illustré, and *L'illustration* fully covered the early events, their photographers recording the activities of the crowds surrounding the building, the police, and the besieged occupants. On orders from their editors to bring back newsworthy pictures of the scene, they even took their cameras and equipment onto the roofs of adjacent buildings and, from this vantage point, took pictures of events on the street and the movements of the leaguers on the roof of the "fort." Understanding the importance of these photographs for his publicity goals, Guérin and his associates gladly accommodated them. Finally police officials realized that he was exploiting the press to his advantage and gave orders to stop all photographers from taking pictures of the scene. Faced with a final ultimatum to surrender, and without any more access to the press, Guérin finally capitulated on September 21.[31]

When Guérin and the other conservative conspirators stood trial in the autumn of 1899 the lessons of this media event in Paris and the Dreyfus trial in Rennes were still fresh in the minds of Republican officials. Prosecution of the defendants took place in the Senate chambers at the Luxembourg Palace, and stringent restrictions were placed on all photographers. No cameramen were permitted in the courtroom itself, and only carefully selected images of the outside environs were allowed. Special windowless cells were constructed deep in the palace for each prisoner so they could not communicate with their followers in the street or be photographed by newsmen below. Even a special covered crossway was constructed that hid the prisoners as they travelled across to the courtroom in the senate chambers.[32]

Censorship in the last half of the nineteenth century had thus evolved from confiscation of individual photographs in circulation to the more fundamental control of the image itself. However, given the growing popularity and industry of photojournalism, this form of censorship would be short lived. Eventually there were simply too many photo-illustrated publications and too many photographers for the authorities to manage. Prevention of press manipulation had to be left to the publications, as editors themselves took on the role of self regulation. Only with the outbreak of war in 1914 would the central

31. APP, BA/1109, Affaire Fort Chabrol, August 29, 1899.
32. Photographers from the illustrated weekly journals were only allowed to take selected pictures of the exterior courtroom and the prisoners' cells. For example, see Léon de Montarlot, "La Haute Cour," *Le monde illustré* (September 23, 1899): 244.

government again attempt systematic censorship of the photographic press.

Looking back today, what subtle or even overt behavioral effects photographs, or any other medium, could have on a viewer is still being debated by scholars and communications experts. What is clear, however, is that when photography was emerging in France as the most popular visual medium of its day, officials in the government clearly thought these images could pose a serious threat to the social and political order. Throughout this period there was a persistent pattern of official surveillance and legal or illegal confiscation of opponents' photographic materials. It is clear that freedom of the press did little to prevent overt censorship by the political authorities when the circumstances demanded it. Only with the vast increase in the number of professional photographers and the reproduction of these pictures in daily newspapers and magazines did it become unsustainable. Advancing technology and modern photojournalism ended the era of official censorship, even if the more basic anxiety of government officials to control the photographic image remained.

KAREN L. CARTER

The Specter of Working-Class Crowds: Political Censorship of Posters in the City of Paris, 1881–1893

> The Poster has been under suspicion, more or less as a matter of prin-
> ciple, right from the start. Its engaging directness, its button-holing
> intrusiveness—and its often appalling bad taste—have engendered in
> the official mind a certain sustained reserve. [. . .] It may be condemned
> as irreverent, indecent, frightening, seditious, controversial, libelous,
> treasonable, offensive, demoralizing, untruthful, immoral, inflamma-
> tory, defamatory.
>
> —Maurice Rickards, 1972[1]

INTRODUCTION

In *The Fall of Public Man*, Richard Sennett describes the changes
in public life and the consideration of urban space that occurred in
Western Europe in the nineteenth century. Instead of the flourishing of vital, thriving spaces of public activity, social interactions,
and engaged human relationships, the withering of public engagement with politics in the modern period resulted in a "dead public
space." This sense of disengagement from public life was particularly acute in the decades after the humiliating defeat of France in
the Franco-Prussian War (1870–1871), the harsh suppression of the
Paris Commune (1871), and the intense commercialization of Paris
following Haussmannization. This development has been analyzed
at this point in historical and art historical scholarship devoted to
fin-de-siècle Paris in no small part because modern writers openly ex-

---

1. Maurice Rickards, *Banned Posters* (Park Ridge, NJ: Noyes Press, 1972), 6–7.
Rickards briefly surveys posters censored for moral reasons, but nevertheless emphasizes the subversive nature of the poster as a visual medium.

YFS 122, *Out of Sight: Political Censorship of the Visual Arts in Nineteenth-Century
France,* ed. Goldstein, © 2012 by Yale University.

pressed their own dissatisfaction and malaise in the post-Commune period.[2]

The reasons for the depoliticization of nineteenth century "public culture" are varied and include the withdrawal of the bourgeoisie from the public sphere, the rise of the commercial mass media, and the advent of popular journalism.[3] Without reducing these arguments to an oversimplification, I would suggest that many scholars, whether they examine these issues by way of theory or via historical evidence, tend to attribute changes in modernity (and its accompanying atomization of the individual) largely to the encroachment of capital into every facet (and space) of daily life.[4] In spite of these overarching economic issues related to the development of capitalism, this essay instead looks at another, less frequently examined cause for the depoliticization of culture and the rise of individual spectatorship: police interference. In the case examined here—political posters displayed in the streets of Paris in the 1880s and 1890s—the deliberate actions of agents of the municipal police and their dispersal of crowds that gathered around posters were attempts to eradicate expressions of political dissent as well as to prevent the collective reading that had historically been associated with the poster.[5]

2. Richard Sennett, *The Fall of Public Man* (New York: W.W. Norton, 1974), 12. Walter Benjamin's essays on Charles Baudelaire, for example, explore this acutely modern awareness of the withering of public space as a consequence of the commercialization of the city. Benjamin, *The Writer of Modern Life: Essays on Charles Baudelaire*, ed. Michael W. Jennings; trans. Howard Eiland et al (Cambridge, MA: Belknap Press, 2006).

3. See especially Sennett, *The Fall of Public Man*; Benjamin, *The Writer of Modern Life: Essays on Charles Baudelaire*; Jürgen Habermas, *The Structural Transformation of the Public Sphere: An Inquiry into a Category of Bourgeois Society*, trans. Thomas Burger (Cambridge, MA: MIT Press, 1992); John Brenkman, "Mass Media: From Collective Experience to the Culture of Privatization," *Social Text: Theory/Culture/Ideology* (Winter 1979), 94–109; *Making the News: Modernity and the Mass Press in Nineteenth-Century France*, ed. Dean de la Motte and Jeanne Przyblyski (Amherst: University of Massachusetts Press, 1999); and David Harvey, *Paris, Capital of Modernity* (New York: Routledge, 2003). Although Brenkman discusses "late" capitalism, the forces of atomization were at work much earlier.

4. One exception is Vanessa Schwartz who interprets late nineteenth-century commercialized entertainment as uniting rather than dividing Parisian audiences. See her *Spectacular Realities: Early Mass Culture in Fin-de-Siècle Paris* (Berkeley: University of California Press, 1998).

5. For information about the political poster in France, see Laurent Gervereau, *La propagande par l'affiche* (Paris: BDIC and Arts Graphiques Modernes, 1991) and Alain Gesgon, *La mémoire murale politique des Français de la Renaissance à nos jours* (Paris: La Conciergerie [exh. cat.], 1984).

As I argue in this essay, it was precisely the revolutionary potential of the poster—established by a legacy of the political poster extending back to the French Revolution—and the poster's mode of collective spectatorship that made it subject to greater scrutiny in the period after the passage of the 1881 Press Law (*loi de presse*, 29 juillet 1881). After 1881, the poster was more likely to reach a broader swath of the public than before, and the Parisian authorities sought to control this collective viewing experience rather than to allow it to percolate into working-class discontent and action. The history of the censorship of the political poster, then, is one of the radical promise of posters as assured by the 1881 Press Law and the dismantling of that potential shortly after its passage. Ultimately, this essay will examine the poster's mode of reception and its political message as having earned its reputation as a subversive object that required surveillance and scrutinizing even after its display had been sanctioned under the new Press Law. That process of surveillance, monitoring, and above all the dispersal of crowds by the Parisian police around posters lead to the decline of the political force of the poster.

LIBERTÉ DE L'AFFICHAGE AND THE PRESS LAW OF 1881

On July 29, 1881 the Third Republic passed the Press Law, a broadly sweeping liberal legislation that was drafted to allow the free exchange of ideas in newspapers, books, and posters that were critical of religious, social, or political groups including the government. It also permitted the *liberté de l'affichage*, or the right of individuals to post bills in public, as long as certain criteria were met. A poster was required to bear the name and address of the printer, be printed on colored paper (because white paper was reserved for government announcements), and display a valid tax stamp; a poster could not condemn or defame specific individuals, spread false news, incite citizens to commit serious crimes, address members of the military, or be posted on walls of prohibited buildings.[6] Just as important as the right

---

6. The 1881 Press Law allowed for specific buildings to be excluded from bill-posting; these were designated by the inscription: "Defense d'afficher par la loi de 29 juillet 1881." Municipal authorities (*maires* or prefects) were still allowed to reserve public walls exclusively for the posting of administrative announcements distributed by the government. For a summary of the 1881 Press Law (including *liberté de l'affichage*) and its subsequent revisions until 1900, see Claude Bellanger, Jacques Godechot et al, *Histoire générale de la presse française* (Paris: Presses Universitaires

to post material, the Press Law specifically protected the poster as an object and banned its willful and malicious destruction.[7] The enormity of this action can only be grasped by pointing out that throughout most of the nineteenth century, the political poster was regarded as so seemingly dangerous in France that it had been banned.[8] After the new Press Law was passed, French citizens could use posters to criticize their government and their fellow citizens, to challenge cherished beliefs and even to denounce the constitution itself.[9]

The ramifications of unobstructed *affichage* as established by the original 1881 Press Law were far-reaching. Since the Press Law

de France, 1972), v. 3, 7–31. For a more thorough list of *affichage* regulations, see Gustave Le Poittevin, *Traité de la presse: Réglementation de l'imprimerie, de la librairie, de la presse périodique, de l'affichage et du colportage et infractions commises par l'impression, l'écriture et la parole*, 3 vols. (Paris: Librairie de la Société du Recueil Général des Lois et des Arrêts, 1901–1903); Édouard Fuzier-Herman and Th. Griffond, *Jurisprudence du XIXe siècle. 4e table décennale, alphabétique et chronologique du recueil général des lois et arrêts (1881 à 1890) présentant, sur toutes les matières du droit, des résumés de la législation* [. . .], ed. Jean-Baptiste Sirey (Paris: Librairie du Recueil général des lois et des arrêts et du Journal du Palais, 1894), 34–7; and Olivier de Gourmont, *Jurisprudence du XIXe siècle. 5e table décennale, alphabétique et chronologique du recueil général des lois et des arrêts (1891 a 1900) présentant, sur toutes les matières du droit, des résumés de la législation* [. . .], ed. Jean-Baptiste Sirey (Paris: Librairie du Recueil général des lois et des arrêts et du Journal du Palais, 1902), 33–34. Paul Bernelle also provides a summary of *affichage* laws in his *Des restrictions apportées depuis 1881 à la liberté de l'affichage, thèse pour le doctorat*, Université de Paris, faculté de droit (Paris: Arthur Rousseau, 1912). In contrast to the vast body of literature that documents the history of book censorship in the nineteenth century, very little has been written about poster censorship. For a recent analysis of censorship of nonpolitical *canards* advertising sensational news, see Thomas J. Cragin, "The Failings of Popular News Censorship in Nineteenth-Century France," *Book History* 4 (2001): 40–80. For an examination of the censorship of publicity posters, see Karen L. Carter, "Unfit for Public Display: Female Sexuality and the Censorship of Fin-de-Siècle Publicity Posters," *Early Popular Visual Culture* 8/ 2 (May 2010): 107–124 and *"L'âge de l'affiche*: Critics, Collectors and Urban Contexts," in *Toulouse-Lautrec and the French Imprint: Sources and Legacies of Fin-de-Siècle Posters, Paris — Brussels — Barcelona*, curated and edited by Dennis Cate (New Brunswick, New Jersey: Jane Voorhees Zimmerli Museum of Art, 2005); Jane Clapp, *Art Censorship: A Chronology of Proscribed and Prescribed Art* (Metuchen, N.J.: The Scarecrow Press, 1972); and Rickards.

7. Le Poittevin, volume II, 307–308.

8. The French state and local authorities held the rights to post announcements, laws, and decrees, but political posters, even simple announcements, had been effectively kept from appearing on city walls through a system of prior approval by the local prefects. Publicity posters were also subject to the same prior approval from roughly 1830 to 1881, but were usually approved.

9. Le Comité des droits de l'homme et du citoyen, *De l'affichage politique, Conseil practiques pour la rédaction, l'apposition et la protection des affiches: jurisprudence et texte de la loi sur la presse* (Montpellier: Gustave Firmin et Montane, 1895), 45.

removed all pre-existing restrictions for *affichage* in the streets, the number of posters pasted on city walls increased exponentially after 1881. As a result, the Parisian authorities, heretofore charged with regulating the placement of mass-distributed posters and with approving their content *before* they could be distributed, were suddenly confronted with a plethora of publicity and political *affiches* that they were seemingly unable (from both a practical and a legal standpoint) to monitor and control.[10] The press, presumably speaking for the public, complained about the overabundance of electoral, commercial, and political posters throughout the 1880s and 1890s.[11] Contemporary images documented unrestrained *affichage* especially during electoral periods (Fig. 1). In addition to complaints about posters desecrating public monuments and buildings, articles in the press expressed anxiety about the poster's imagined negative consequences including threats to the stability of the Third Republic, incitements to illegal behavior, and urban violence.

Republicans initially were reluctant to impede the absolute principles of freedom of expression that were guaranteed by the 1881 Law. As the press was increasingly perceived as a formidable and even potentially disruptive force, legislators supported attempts to revise the Press Laws in order to suppress politically extreme viewpoints. By exerting more control over the French press, Republicans were responding equally to pressure from their more conservative colleagues to curb the distribution of ostensibly inflammatory political posters. Credited with disseminating political information that had

10. Although other French cities experienced the same difficulties regulating posters, the focus here is only on the city of Paris. The more advanced state of publicity in the capital and the larger number of posters distributed there justify this choice of Paris as the model for gauging reactions to publicity and propaganda posters.

11. Many journalists complained about the problem of electoral posters littering the streets. See, for example, Felicien Champsaur, "Jules Chéret," *L'événement* (Sept. 19, 1889) and Lionel Mogues, "Le Mur et l'affiche," *L'événement* (Sept. 22, 1889) : 2. According to Le Poittevin, there were virtually no restraints placed on electoral posters ("professions of faith" with the candidate's name) in the 1880s and 1890s, except that candidates could not post bills on the official *emplacements* reserved by municipalities for laws, announcements, and decrees (Le Poittevin, v. II, 298). The prohibition of *affichage* on buildings of artistic importance was not established until 1902 (law of January 27, 1902), Le Poittevin, volume. II, 298–99. Subsequent laws in 1914 and 1935 confined the posting of electoral posters to panels provided outside neighborhood polling places. See also Gabrielle Trouillard-Perrot, *L'affichage et l'esthétique: De la loi du 20 juillet 1881 sur la liberté de la Presse au décret-loi du 30 octobre 1935 contre les abus de l'affichage et à la loi des Finances du 31 décembre 1938* (Paris: Librairie Sociale et Économique, 1940).

PARIS. — L'AFFICHAGE PENDANT LES ÉLECTIONS LÉGISLATIVES DU 8 MAI. — (Photographies de M. Gaillard, gravure de Reymond.)
Voir page 315.

Figure 1. M. Gaillard and M. Reymond, "Paris – L'affichage pendant les élections législatives du 8 mai," *L'univers illustré* (May 14, 1898): 313. Courtesy of the Bibliothèque nationale de France. FOL- LC2- 2956, n° 2251.

previously been prohibited, posters, some conservatives argued, were responsible for the increase in workers' protests and riots and therefore required careful regulation, if not outright prohibition.[12]

In the years following the 1881 Press Law revisions were added to the original statute in order to address recent "crises" of public dissemination of information. In the end, greater bureaucratic regulation and surveillance were the ultimate consequences of the Law. Press infractions, newly established by subsequent revisions to the 1881 Law, usually did not carry prison sentences, but were nevertheless designed to limit press liberty.[13] This shift away from a policy of absolute press freedom to one of greater regulation followed a series of political crises in which the press played a key role in galvanizing public opinion against the Republicans; the elections of 1885 and the Boulangist crisis were two such incidents in which Republicans were the subject of negative propaganda.[14] Therefore, after enduring challenges to the Third Republic's own political stability, the same group largely responsible for press liberalization eventually advocated its restriction.

The law was first amended to counter the marked dissemination of salacious texts and images that flooded the city streets in 1881, referred to as "the year of pornography."[15] The subsequent August 2, 1882 revision to the Press Law addressed *outrage aux bonnes moeurs* (violations of public decency) and was used to condemn publicity posters that advertised a spate of anti-clerical tracts, journals, books, and posters that viciously condemned the Pope and the Catholic Church.[16] Proposals to restrict the right to defame the government were attempted following the distribution of printed material by Prince Jérôme Bonaparte in 1883 (discussed below) and General Boulanger in 1889, but not ultimately passed.[17] In all these notorious

12. This viewpoint is borne out by articles in the conservative press. Articles in the conservative *Le temps* heavily criticized the "incomprehensible and insufficient" Press Law and called for outright suppression of seditious posters, emblems, and slogans. *Le temps* (April 13 and June 28, 1886).

13. Bellanger and Godechot, 23.

14. Bellanger and Godechot, 245. "After the elections of 1885 and the Boulanger crisis, Republicans quickly realized that, contrary to their illusions in 1881, propaganda by the press could pose serious dangers to the Republic itself."

15. Léon Sabatié, *La censure* (Paris: Pedone, 1908): 128.

16. For a partial list of illustrated anti-clerical posters that were censored in 1883–1887, see Henri Béraldi, *Les graveurs du XIXe siècle: guide de l'amateur d'estampes* (Nogent-le-Roi: Lame, 1981; orig. 1885–92) v. 4, 17–18.

17. Bellanger and Godechot, 24.

cases, the poster was regarded as a key element if not a prime instigator of crises of confidence in press liberalization. As early as 1883, the jurist and legal scholar Georges Barbier wrote in his Introduction to the Press Code (*Code de la Presse*) that within the eighteen months following the Law's passage so many changes had been enacted that press freedom had been compromised.[18]

The most severe limitations to press freedom were enacted in 1893 and 1894 by way of the so-called *lois scélérates*, three separate laws passed in the wake of several recent bombings and the assassination of President Carnot. Designed to crack down on anarchist activity, the first law forbade the incitement of criminal acts, the second proscribed association with those intending to do harm, and the third law—especially pertinent for the distribution of political posters—prohibited anarchist propaganda "by any means" whatsoever.[19] This last law was ultimately used to repress socialist as well as anarchist propaganda, effectively ending a ten-year period of legalized distribution of radical political posters and thereby reinstating a policy that was based on the conception of political posters as having the power to incite social unrest and violence.

Therefore, despite the far-reaching consequences for the expression of political views in public, the Press Law did not completely ensure the free exchange of political ideas in the streets, but ushered in a new, typically modern manifestation of censorship in which specific examples of "seditious" material were singled out for scrutiny in the midst of a flood of published material.[20] Hardly monolithic and seldom consistent, censorship of political posters during this period was distinguished less by prolonged periods of repression, as had been the case in the past, and could be characterized more by intense, albeit brief moments of censorship focused on individual examples

18. "After scarcely eighteen months had passed, modifications to restrict the freedom of the law were already being considered." Reprinted in Bellanger and Godechot, 23–24.

19. Joan Halperin, *Felix Fénéon: Aesthete and Anarchist in Fin-de-Siècle Paris* (New Haven: Yale University Press, 1988), 271.

20. France was certainly not the most restrictive of European nations during this period. In terms of the quantity of material seized by the government for political reasons, Austria and Russia were probably the worst offenders. See Robert Goldstein, *Political Censorship of the Arts and the Press in Nineteenth-Century Europe* (London: Macmillan, 1989). For an analysis of the censorship of political caricature, see also his "Censorship of Caricature in France, 1815–1914," *French History* 3/1(March 1989): 71–107 and "The Debate over Censorship of Caricature in Nineteenth-Century France," *Art Journal* 48/1 (Spring 1989): 9–15.

that were confiscated after public outcry or, more frequently, police surveillance.

THE SUBVERSIVE CHARACTER OF THE POSTER

During the period examined here (1881–1893), the police engaged in an elaborate system of surveillance and confiscation of political posters—even in this period of presumed freedom of *affichage*—in part because of the historical and contemporary conceptions of the role that posters played in the propagation of radical ideas and popular discontent. The type of spectatorship associated with textual posters was the collective reading that was expected of all posters, but was especially associated with political broadsides that were displayed in public places. Although political posters were prohibited for most of the late eighteenth and nineteenth centuries, in periods of popular uprisings and rebellions, such as the French Revolution, the Revolution of 1848 and the Paris Commune, *liberté de l'affichage* was established and the censorship that kept political *placards* off the walls of French cities was eliminated, however briefly.[21]

Although in the pre-modern era, the majority of posters distributed contained administrative or religious content and served as a means of informing the public of recent edicts and ordinances, *placards* and *canards*—the precursors of modern political posters—were linked with "popular" political opinion and were often critical of local or national figures. Considered a "spontaneous form of expression," these *placards*—both printed and handwritten—often appeared during periods of economic crisis or rebellion.[22] For much of the eighteenth century, this view of the poster as potentially subversive and representative of popular, urban culture continued to persist and culminated with the French Revolution. In *The People of Paris*, Daniel Roche character-

21. Indeed, the Revolution marked the first time in French history that posters could be distributed without prior consent as three successive laws—dating from 1789, 1790, and 1791—permitted the posting of newspaper pages and political *placards* on public walls. Other subsequent French governments had granted the public the freedom to freely distribute posters (*liberté de l'affichage*) for 6 months at the beginning of the July Monarchy, briefly in 1848 and, again, briefly under the Paris Commune in 1871. See especially Bernelle, 11–16.

22. Christian Jouhard, "Readability and Persuasion: Political Handbills," in Roger Chartier, ed. *The Cultural Uses of Print in Early Modern Europe*, trans. Lydia Cochrane (Princeton, NJ: Princeton University Press, 1987), 235.

izes the poster as "a book for all to read."[23] Although most eighteenth-century posters were bureaucratic in content, they were equally perceived, Roche states, as exemplifying the only medium "that enabled the popular classes to express their opinion of political life."[24] In addition to its reputation as possibly seditious, the poster offered all classes of the city an opportunity to keep informed of the latest news free of charge.[25] If spectators could not grasp the content of a poster from its capitalized letters and images, they could glean its meaning from other citizens who gathered around it and read aloud.[26] This communal consumption of political posters was vital during the Revolution as a way to inform the urban public and to disseminate political information. Although other public institutions, especially public reading rooms, existed for the collective reading of newspapers and books before the nineteenth century, none matched the accessibility of the poster.[27]

The political poster continued to be associated with revolutionary ideas and with the urban working class during the nineteenth century. In two articles published in *Neue Rheinische Zeitung* in 1849, Frederick Engels advocated "the right of workers to the *literature provided free of charge* in the form of posters" and championed the poster as the "chief means of influencing the proletariat."[28] Engels stated:

23. Daniel Roche, *The People of Paris: An Essay in Popular Culture in the Eighteenth Century* (New York: Berg, 1987), 229.

24. Roche, 230. According to Roche, the majority of announcements posted were proclamations distributed by the Crown, the Church or the local police. Wedding and death announcements would have been interspersed with these official *placards* on the walls of Paris.

25. According to Roche, the police also searched walls for seditious material in the eighteenth century (Roche, 230).

26. Roche, 228. Roche claims that the proliferation of political posters in the pre-revolutionary period was somewhat limited; however, two key episodes reinforced the view of posters as inflammatory: 1725–30 during the "Jansenist troubles," and 1768–75, a period of economic and political crisis (Roche, 230).

27. Although collective reading, rather than private ownership of reading material, was the rule rather than the exception in eighteenth-century France, no other reading environment offered the same experience as did the reading of posters in the streets. Public libraries offered the lending of books and spaces to read, but rarely possessed the same types of daily and weekly newspapers that were posted on walls. See Roger Chartier, "Urban Reading and Practices, 1660–1780," in *The Cultural Uses of Print*, 183–239. For information about the consumption of periodicals in Revolutionary France, see Jeremy Popkin, *Revolutionary News: The Press in France, 1789–1799* (Durham, NC: Duke University Press, 1990).

28. Frederick Engels, "The Debate on the Law on Posters," *Neue Rheinische Zeitung* (April 22 and 27, 1849) reprinted in *Karl Marx, Frederick Engels, Collected Works,*

And what is more conducive to keeping the revolutionary fervor alive among the workers than posters, which convert every street corner into a huge newspaper in which workers who pass by find the events of the day noted and commented on, the various views described and discussed, and where at the same time they meet people of all classes and opinions with whom they can discuss the contents of posters; in short, where they have simultaneously a newspaper and a club, and all without costing them a penny![29]

Engels was reporting on the recent debates held in Germany about the censorship of posters, but his reportage presents us with commonly held assumptions about the poster in nineteenth-century Europe. He quotes the remarks of the politician Herr Riedel who on the one hand advocated for better access to information but, on the other, argued for restrictions on the proliferation of political posters. Riedel stated:

As a rule, posters serve merely to inflame *passions*, to kindle an *impure fire of hatred* or *revenge* particularly against the authorities [. . .] As a rule, therefore, posters are precisely the opposite of what their name implies. Hence their use is usually a misuse and therefore the question arises: Ought the police authorities help promote this mischief of posters?[30]

In Engels's opinion, opponents of the poster were usually in favor of press freedom for the bourgeoisie but sought to restrict posters precisely because of their appeal to urban workers.[31] The singling out of the political poster as a special case in Germany, according to Engels, was part of an "outright appeal to the fears of the propertied classes" that posters would, in the words of Riedel, "serve as a call to the *unreasoning mass* to demonstrations which menacingly violate order and go beyond the limits of legitimate freedom."[32] According to En-

---

v. 9, trans. Richard Dixon and others (New York: International Publishers, 1977): 320–329, cited on 323–24. Italics are provided in the published English version. I am grateful to Claudia Mesch for pointing out this reference to me.

29. Engels, 326.

30. Engels, 325. Orig. pub. in *Neue Rheinische Zeitung* 283 (April 27, 1849). Engels inserts his own remarks (removed here) into this quote in which he emphasizes that Riedel objected to the posting of political tracts because they were not by definition posters (*placards*), which he presumably considered information or, in Engels's words, "reassuring tracts" instead of anti-government opinions. Emphasis added by Engels.

31. Engels, 324.

32. Engels, 325.

gels, the censorship of political posters had at the heart of its motives the "stifling of class struggle, the gagging of the oppressed classes."[33]

By the late nineteenth century, the perception of the poster as a rallying point for the proletariat and a mouthpiece of radical politics was commonplace. The so-called Moral Order (1871–1879) in France allowed the posting of political materials only if they had been given prior approval; this prohibition simply followed the policy of the Second Empire.[34] Newspaper articles of the 1880s also made the connection between political posters and crowd action especially during workers' strikes and protests.[35] Therefore, the specter of crowds gathered around posters discussing their political content proved so threatening as to warrant the greater scrutiny of political posters in the decades following the Paris Commune.[36]

SEDITIOUS POSTERS CENSORED IN THE CITY OF PARIS, 1881–1893

While in principle the 1881 Press Law permitted the streets of Paris to be a site for the open expression of politically diverse opinions, in practice local authorities confiscated political posters pasted on city walls for the sake of "public safety" and "public decency" often under orders from the Minister of Justice, or the local prefect, or in response

33. Engels, 327.

34. For an examination of the conservative policies at the beginning of the Third Republic, see Jean-Marie Mayeur and Madeleine Rebérioux, *The Third Republic from its Origins to the Great War, 1871–1914*, trans. J. R. Foster (Cambridge: Cambridge University Press,1989).

35. An article in *Le temps* mentioned both the positive and negative roles played by posters in the strikes at Decazeville: "Au Jour le Jour: La grève de Decazeville," *Le temps* (April 9, 1886): 2. Another article, which was published after the distribution of posters by the comte de Paris and a legislative attempt to restrict *affichage*, made the connection between the posting of political material and disorder in the streets: "We recognize however that this precaution is not useless for the future, since in some circumstances the display of a poster can be the cause of danger, or at least disorder, in the street." The article goes on to suggest that the more "frequent" harm could be caused by the shouting of seditious slogans and illegal emblems, two other types of provocative material that the police already monitored. *Le temps* (June 28, 1886): 1.

36. For an inventory of Paris Commune posters in the collection of the French National Archives, see Marie-Christine Moine, *Affiches imprimées, 19e-20e siècles: Révolution de 1848, gouvernement de la Défense nationale (1870–1871), Commune de Paris (1871), Guerre de 1914–1918, Archives nationales inventaire analytique des articles AD XXe 77, 79 à 88*, ed. Odile Krakovitch with a preface by Jean Favier (Paris: National Archives, 1992).

to complaints from residents.[37] The frequency with which the police monitored and confiscated political *placards* indicates that the new legislation, far from eliminating political censorship altogether, in essence complicated its practice by the fact that the police were forbidden to halt in any way the *distribution* of a given poster even if it violated an existing law. The confiscation and destruction of condemned posters could be accomplished only *after* its public display.[38] Both of these rationales, public safety and decency, were used as reasons to sacrifice the plurality of political viewpoints in the years following the new Press Law. [39]

As mentioned earlier, the political force of the poster declined after the passage of the 1881 Press Law that was initially passed as part of a larger program of press liberalization under the Third Republic. And while the greater bureaucratization of poster regulation had resulted in a decline in *liberté de l'affichage*, the political potential of the poster was ever more stifled through the actions of the Parisian

37. Michel Melot also identifies public decency and public safety as challenges to press freedom for printmaking in France after 1881. Melot, "The Image in France," in *Censorship: 500 Years of Conflict* (New York: The New York Public Library, 1984), 89.

38. Le comité des droits de l'homme et du citoyen, *De l'affichage politique, Conseil practiques pour la rédaction, l'apposition et la protection des affiches: jurisprudence et texte de la loi sur la presse* (Montpellier: Gustave Firmin et Montane, 1895), 17. Hereafter cited as *De l'affichage politique*. Trouillard-Perrot, 8. For information on police procedures and censored posters, see the Archives de la Préfecture de Police, Paris (hereafter cited as APP), especially dossiers BA 472: *Inscriptions et placards séditeux ou injurieux, 1880–1893*; BA 476: *Placards injurieux ou obscène, 1872, 1873, 1874*; BA 478: *Placards injurieux ou obscènes, 1880–1888* and BA 479: *Placards injurieux ou obscènes, 1883* and BA 640: *Elections législatives, affiches*, 1889. Much of the information included in this article concerning the censorship of political posters has been culled for the daily reports in the Police Archives and from newspaper articles. According to Bellanger and Godechot, the dossiers for the Minister of the Interior for this period (series F7 and F18 of the Archives nationales) contain few relevant documents and those that survive are in particularly poor condition (Bellanger, 146). For a summary in English of the contents of this archive and its relevance for historical research after 1871, see Marvin Brown, "Archives de la Prefecture de Police," *French Historical Studies* 4/4 (Autumn 1966): 463–67.

39. Although the police were forbidden from confiscating material on their own initiative—posters could be seized only if a magistrate decreed it—several initiatives were proposed during the 1880s to restore the authority of the police to determine what material could be posted. See articles in *Le temps*, 1883–1888. Posters could equally be confiscated, torn down or pasted over if they constituted a danger or a public threat to "a sense of decency." *De l'affichage politique*, 21.

police force that sought to quell popular dissent.[40] The Parisian police's policy of surveillance and restriction was not as repressive as the prior approval required by the Second Empire, but it presented in many ways a continuation of that regime's distrust of the working class, their establishments and gathering places. The monitoring of political posters and their eventual censorship, therefore, can be regarded as another attempt of the Third Republic to control and monitor working-class sociability and political activity.[41]

Instead of exerting absolute authority over the distribution of posters, the Parisian police engaged in the nightly routine of monitoring city streets for examples of material they believed was seditious—posters, handwritten notes, and even graffiti scratched into walls and monuments. Sometimes these nightly patrols meant only an alert of potential disruptions and other times included the effacement of inscriptions, the destruction of *placards*, and the dispersal of small gatherings of people in pre-emptive acts justified by the need for public safety. Over time, however, these small acts, often committed in the dark of night with an eye to avoiding public attention, and carried out virtually every day for over a decade, led to the depoliticization of the poster and therefore its decline as an instrument for revolution. [42]

The confiscation of political propaganda was often the result of the police's continued surveillance of neighborhoods associated with working-class residents, transient populations, and illicit prostitu-

40. The term "police" in this essay is used to designate the various branches of the municipal and national police force that was under the jurisdiction of the Parisian police prefect (*police simple, gardiens de la paix, gendarmerie, agents des garnis, service en bourgeois*) who acted in concert, along with shop owners and landlords, to monitor and report posters suspected of sedition, especially if crowds gathered around them.

41. According to Susanna Barrows, restrictions on drinking and gathering in *débits de boisson* immediately following the Commune also prohibited patrons from reading newspapers aloud or posting electoral posters. Barrows, "Nineteenth-Century Cafés: Arenas of Everyday Life" in *Pleasures of Paris, Daumier to Picasso*, ed. Barbara Stern Shapiro with the assistance of Anne E. Havinga (Boston: Museum of Fine Arts, Boston and D.R. Godine, 1991), 17–26. For information about the restrictions placed on cafés, see Adrian Rifkin, "Cultural Movement and the Paris Commune," *Art History* 2/2 (June 1979): 201–20 and W. Scott Haine, *The World of the Paris Café: Sociability among the French Working Class, 1789–1914* (Baltimore, MD: The Johns Hopkins University Press, 1998).

42. By the end of the 1880s, most critics regarded the viewership of all posters as performed by an individual rather than a crowd in the streets.

tion.[43] The records of the Parisian police prefect clearly articulate the rational for destroying posters if a crowd formed. For example, police reports of November 5, 1882 and February 13, 1883 clearly stated that officers destroyed posters in order to disperse crowds that had formed around them.[44] The police records for seditious posters are filled with references to the number of pedestrians who gathered in front of posters, their comments and their general mood about the destruction of radical propaganda.[45] Even if a poster were merely an announcement, such as the poster advertising "Grande Réunion" (Fig. 2), the authorities could literally "see red" and destroy it in the name of public safety.[46]

Usually both the confiscation and distribution of political posters were clandestine activities completed in the dark of night when billposters pasted up printed material. Police agents, acutely conscious of the power of posters to attract and hold the attention of crowds, tore down "injurious" or "seditious" posters and notices during nightly patrols, before any citizens could view them in the early hours of the morning.[47] Although many billposters (*afficheurs*) worked for publishers and sometimes unwittingly distributed transgressive posters, other renegade *afficheurs* were members of political groups who distributed their own propaganda. Fully aware that police agents searched for seditious material during their neighborhood surveillance, nocturnal *afficheurs* usually posted material between

43. One poster found in the seventeenth arrondissement complained of the Third Republic's policy of legalized prostitution that, according to the *placard*, victimized the working class. APP 472, no. 15 (March 25, 1882). Another report stated that agents in the ninth, tenth, eleventh, eighteenth, nineteenth and twentieth arrondissements had specifically targeted those *quartiers* for seditious posters (APP BA 478, no. 2394).

44. APP BA 472, no. 30 and APP, BA 472, nos. 41–44.

45. See for example, APP BA 472, nos. 44, 45 (March 5, 1883), 48 (March 6, 1883), 66 (May 26, 1884); APP BA 478 nos. 2206, 2277, 2351 (Oct. 26, 1882) and 3202.

46. This poster does mention the "lutte contre les coalitions patronales et capitalistes." Like many socialist posters, this *affiche* was printed on red paper although its color has faded over time. The color red has a long history of being linked to radical politics and its use for certain objects was banned during the Moral Order because of its association with the Commune. See Fernand Drujon, *Catalogue des ouvrages, écrits et dessins de toute nature poursuivis, supprimés ou condamnés depuis le 21 octobre 1814 jusqu'au 31 juillet 1877* (Paris: Librairie ancienne et moderne Édouard Rouveyre, 1879), xxv.

47. According to APP records, the Parisian police also cleaned up any politically extreme (or simply anti-Republican) graffiti that had been scratched or written on walls.

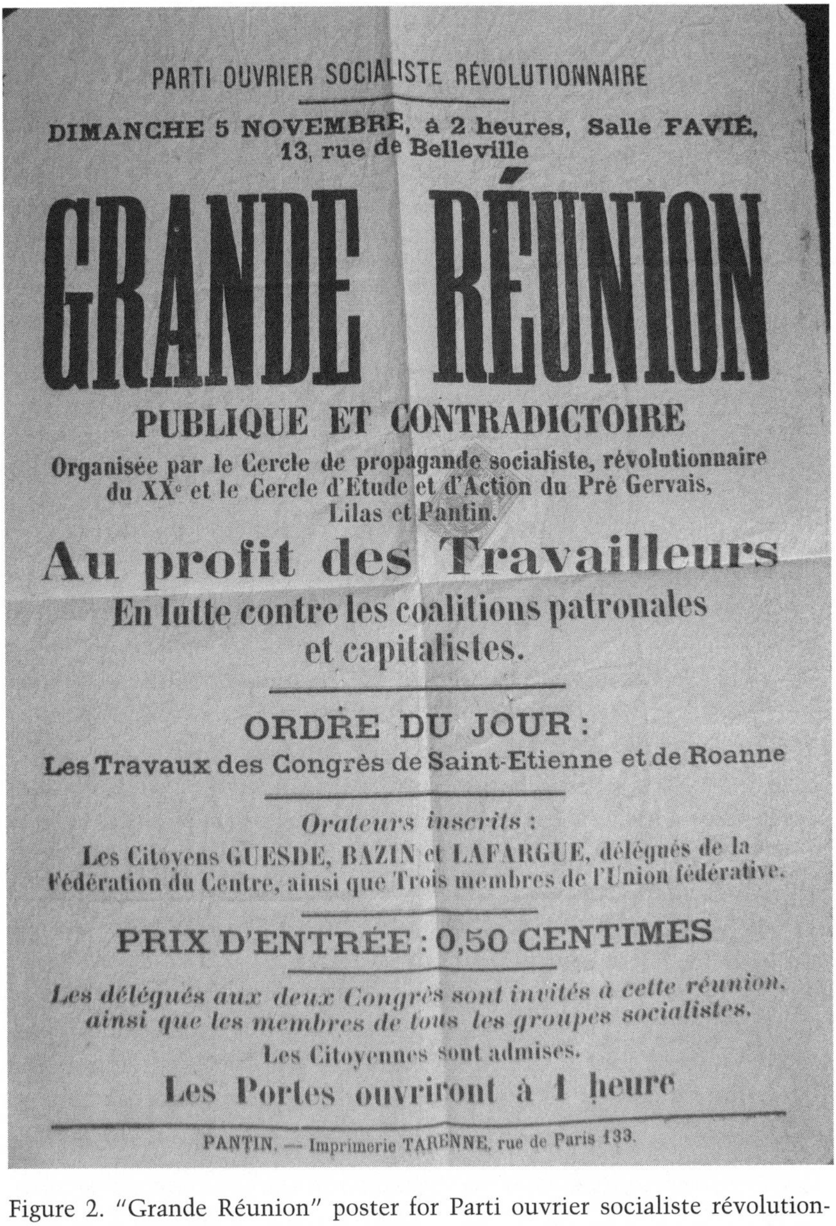

PARTI OUVRIER SOCIALISTE RÉVOLUTIONNAIRE

DIMANCHE 5 NOVEMBRE, à 2 heures, Salle FAVIÉ,
13, rue de Belleville

GRANDE RÉUNION

PUBLIQUE ET CONTRADICTOIRE

Organisée par le Cercle de propagande socialiste, révolutionnaire
du XXᵉ et le Cercle d'Étude et d'Action du Pré Gervais,
Lilas et Pantin.

Au profit des Travailleurs

En lutte contre les coalitions patronales
et capitalistes.

ORDRE DU JOUR :

Les Travaux des Congrès de Saint-Etienne et de Roanne

Orateurs inscrits :
Les Citoyens GUESDE, BAZIN et LAFARGUE, délégués de la
Fédération du Centre, ainsi que Trois membres de l'Union fédérative.

PRIX D'ENTRÉE : 0,50 CENTIMES

*Les délégués aux deux Congrès sont invités à cette réunion,
ainsi que les membres de tous les groupes socialistes.*
Les Citoyennes sont admises.
Les Portes ouvriront à 1 heure

PANTIN. — Imprimerie TARENNE, rue de Paris 133.

Figure 2. "Grande Réunion" poster for Parti ouvrier socialiste révolutionnaire, November 1882. Archives de la Préfecture de Police de Paris, BA 472,
no. 29. © Préfecture de Police. All rights reserved.

three and five in the morning, used special glue that was difficult to remove, and were frequently armed. [48]

Joan Halperin relates an incident of clandestine *affichage* from the point of view of a political activist in her study of anarchist art critic and editor Félix Fénéon:

> He [Fénéon] was also accomplished in plastering up [. . .] posters on the walls of Paris in the dead of night. These were announcements of meetings or anarchist slogans, printed, one of his friends recalled, in flaming red, shrill yellow and hot orange, with gigantic letters to catch the eye. One such manifesto, called "Panama and Dynamite," denounced the financial shenanigans of members of parliament [. . .]. One winter night Fénéon and two helpers covered the walls and fences in Montmartre with this poster [. . .]. The three of them prowled the streets like young pranksters, but more stealthily [. . .]. The trick was to plaster "Panama and Dynamite" high on the walls out of reach of the gendarmes. They were successful, and Montmartre wore her new face for several days, until another poster went up.[49]

The censorship cases in the Police Prefect files usually involved political posters that were openly hostile to the Third Republic or to the middle class. Possibly one of the most notorious cases of seditious propaganda accused of appealing to crowds involved an 1883 Bonapartist poster that was distributed throughout the *quartiers* of Paris (Fig. 3). First pasted up on January 15, 1883, the poster was immediately brought to the attention of the police. One day later, the police arrested Prince Jérôme (Prince Napoléon Joseph Charles Paul Bonaparte, aka "Plon-Plon," 1822–1891), the author of the poster, as well as nine employees of an *affichage* firm as they were pasting up copies of the poster. Printed on bright yellow paper (which has faded over time) and bearing the heading "A mes concitoyens / La République languit," the poster sharply criticized the decline of France under the current Republican government and praised the grandeur of the Empire under Napoleon.[50] The incident created a scandal because

48. The police gleaned this information from interviews of prisoners recently arrested for posting propaganda in October 1882 (APP BA 478, no. 2516, dated November 6, 1882). One "Laroque," a bakery worker who was arrested, claimed that he had narrowly escaped the police two times before and that during his nightly *affichage* sessions he often carried a knife that he would have used to kill a police agent if given the chance.

49. Halperin, 262.

50. APP, BA 472, no. 33. A report dated January 16, 1883 details the arrest of a professional *afficheur* (bill poster) who was caught along with others who were distributing hundreds of these posters.

Figure 3. "A mes concitoyens" manifesto (dated January 15, 1883) distributed by Prince Napoléon Joseph Charles Paul Bonaparte, called Prince Jérôme (1822–1891, aka "Plon-Plon"), censored Jan. 16, 1883 and after. Archives de la Préfecture de Police, Paris, BA 472, no. 35. © Préfecture de Police. All rights reserved.

Prince Jérôme was viewed by Republican politicians as amassing a political attack on the Republic.

While both the domestic and international press portrayed the posting of "Plon-Plon's manifesto" as, at most, a botched attempt to position himself as the Bonapartist pretender (instead of his son, Prince Victor), the Republic continued to view Prince Jérôme (and later the Comte de Paris) and his posters as real threats to the Republic.[51] Shortly thereafter, Monarchist posters that were deemed equally seditious appeared in the streets of Paris and were censored by the police (Fig. 4, "La Ligue Populaire Aux Royalistes"). These events culminated in 1886 when all pretenders, Bourbon and Bonapartist, were expelled from France in the name of security for the Republic.[52]

An illustrated cover of *L'illustration* depicts the events of January 15 and portrays what the authorities had seemingly feared with large segments of the working-class population collectively reading the extreme viewpoints expressed in Prince Jérôme's *placards* (Fig. 5). Although this assembly of ostensibly peaceful citizens hardly seems threatening, the image visually captures a common conception of political posters as verbal incitements and physical rallying points for the working class.[53] The Republic, and the Parisian police, however, were deadly serious about the seditious quality of these posters and went to the extreme of censoring an advertising poster for a local hat maker that merely spoofed Prince Jérôme's manifesto.[54]

---

51. "Plon-Plon's Manifesto," *The New York Times*, Jan. 17, 1883. This article claimed that "the French republic is in no danger from 'Plon-Plon' but the government's handling of this case lent Prince Jérôme more credibility than he deserved."

52. "The Exiled Pretenders: Arrival of the Comte de Paris in England," *The New York Times* (June 25, 1886).

53. Police records noted the formation of crowds around posters protesting the expulsion of the princes d'Orléans from the French army: "The crowds that gather in front of these posters give rise to various commentaries." (BA 472, no. 45, March 5, 1883). Political posters were only one form of potentially inflammatory material that was singled out for official scrutiny during this period. Following incidents of false news and lewd remarks shouted in public, the state attempted to institute greater control over those who made their living selling publications in the streets. The Minister of the Interior planned to draft a law that would regulate what remarks vendors could call out when selling newspapers. The new ordinance, drafted specifically to restrict the hawking of news in public thoroughfares, was justified by the Minister of the Interior as necessary for public safety. "Les crieurs de journaux," *Lanterne* (March 17, 1887) from APP BA 478, no. 3417.

54. APP BA 472, nos. 37 and 38.

LA LIGUE POPULAIRE

Aux Royalistes

En présence des efforts de la presse républicaine pour jeter de nouveau la division et le désarroi dans le camp royaliste, le Comité-Directeur de la *Ligue populaire* croit de son devoir d'élever la voix. S'il peut, au point de vue des détails, s'élever quelquefois des discussions entre les différents groupes royalistes, ceux-ci sont tous étroitement unis par les principes fondamentaux qui font la base de leurs convictions.

Leur programme, à *tous*, est celui de M. le comte de Chambord, le chef de cette maison de France réconciliée dans le seul but de rendre à notre pays son rang, sa prospérité, sa gloire et sa grandeur.

Et pour tout homme de bonne foi, il ne peut y avoir d'équivoque.

La monarchie française sera l'alliance assurée d'une autorité forte et d'une sage liberté ; c'est-à-dire le gouvernement représentatif dans sa puissante vitalité avec le secours de deux chambres dont l'une sera nommée par le souverain dans des catégories déterminées, l'autre par la nation à l'aide du suffrage universel honnêtement pratiqué ; c'est-à-dire encore, les dépenses publiques sérieusement contrôlées, le libre accès de chacun aux emplois et aux honneurs ; la liberté religieuse, les libertés civiles, la liberté d'enseignement consacrées et hors d'atteinte ; la propriété foncière rendue à la vie et à l'indépendance par la diminution des charges qui pèsent sur elle ; l'association ouvrière opposée à l'individualisme ; les corporations libres opposées au privilège industriel ; l'agriculture, le commerce, l'industrie constamment encouragés et défendus contre la concurrence étrangère.

Et au-dessus de tout cela, l'honnêteté, comme l'a si bien dit le roi, l'honnêteté qui n'est pas moins une obligation dans la vie publique que dans la vie privée, l'honnêteté qui fait la valeur morale des États comme des particuliers.

Voilà les garanties de la monarchie, de la monarchie véritable, de la monarchie traditionnelle qui, par sa situation et les alliances de ses représentants, peut seule assurer une paix durable à la France et lui rendre son intégrité sans le secours de la guerre ; de cette monarchie qui n'a ni fortune à refaire, ni ambition à assouvir ; de la monarchie qui nous débarrassera de ces impuissants qui ne savent que flatter ou tromper le peuple qu'ils appellent à eux.

+ Au milieu des crises que nous traversons, le salut ne peut venir que de cette grande maison de France dont tous les princes ont si bien compris leur devoir en accomplissant l'acte mémorable du 5 août 1873.

Français, rallions-nous confiants derrière eux.

Vive Henri V, Vive le Comte de Paris.

Pour le Comité :

Les Délégués :

Adolphe PIEYRE, député ; Georges BERRY ; Charles NICOULLAUD.

Figure 4. "La Ligue Populaire / Aux Royalistes . . . Vive Henri V, Vive le Comte de Paris" (The Popular League of Royalists . . . Long live Henri V, Long live the Count of Paris), censored poster, c. 1883, Archives de la Préfecture de Police, Paris, BA 472, no. 54. © Préfecture de Police. All rights reserved.

Figure 5. F. Meaulle, *Le Manifeste du Prince Napoléon: La lecture des affiches, le 15 janvier, sur les murs de Paris.* Cover of *L'illustration* (January 27, 1883). Photograph courtesy of The Joseph Regenstein Library, The University of Chicago.

Despite these confiscations of Monarchist and Bonapartist propaganda, the majority of posters censored by the Parisian police in the ten-year period following the passage of the new Press Law tended to be associated with anarchism or socialism. Some of these placards were hand-written announcements that seem more the work of desperate individuals than the manifestos of highly organized groups bent on toppling the current government, attacking the middle class and enacting class warfare (Figs. 6–8: "Mort aux Propriètaires" and "Vive La Revolution" and "Avis / Prolétaires! Esclaves du capital!"). At their most basic element, they express working-class discontent and communicate a sense of violent anger directed at the "haves" by the "have nots."[55] In 1882, the police focused attempts to arrest those responsible for distributing a printed anarchist poster, with the heading "Mort aux voleurs!" (Fig. 9).[56] The "thieves" named in this poster included merchants, industrialists, the clergy, the police, and all property owners. Although objections to the concept of property were protected by the Press Law, the police regularly noted in their daily reports if a seized poster criticized property owners and transcribed verbatim the texts of any poster that might be perceived as threatening to the middle class and public institutions or called for the unification of the popular masses.[57]

Two other posters dating from 1882 ascribed to the Executive Committee of International Revolutionaries (*Comité exécutif*

55. Despite the homemade appearance of these posters, they were still reported in the press. "Les Placards à Paris," *Clairon* (Oct. 29, 1882) noted that copies of the "Avis / Prolétaires, esclaves du capital" posters were found in the sixth and tenth arrondissements. Notices were also included in *Constitutionnel* (Oct. 29, 1882) and *Le soir* (Oct. 22, 1882). *Le soir* claimed that the posters, displayed in the "quartiers populeux" were used as provocation on the part of conservatives to criticize the Republic and to ignite civil war. A more paranoid view was taken by *Le mot d'ordre* (Oct. 22, 1882; APP BA 478, no. 2231) that claimed the revolutionary posters were actually the work of a "politicized" police force that intended to create public fear.

56. APP, BA 472, documents dating from June 1882. Hardly an eye-catching piece of political propaganda, the "poster" is actually the first page of a newspaper, comprised of four columns of printed text with a small printed image of a skull. The dossier contains several copies of this poster, still stiffened with glue, suggesting that they were indeed carefully removed from walls and then put in police files for evidence. According to the printer's address, this poster ("Mort aux voleurs!") ("Death to the Thieves!") was printed in Geneva. It was a common strategy of radical groups to print potentially inflammatory material in foreign countries where printers were out of reach of the local police.

57. Often radical posters were torn down at the request of a local resident or reported to the police by a postal carrier or *concierge*.

Figure 6. "Mort aux Propriètaires [sic]" (Death to Property Owners/Landlords), Censored poster, Archives de la Préfecture de Police, Paris, BA 478, no. 2297. © Préfecture de Police. All rights reserved.

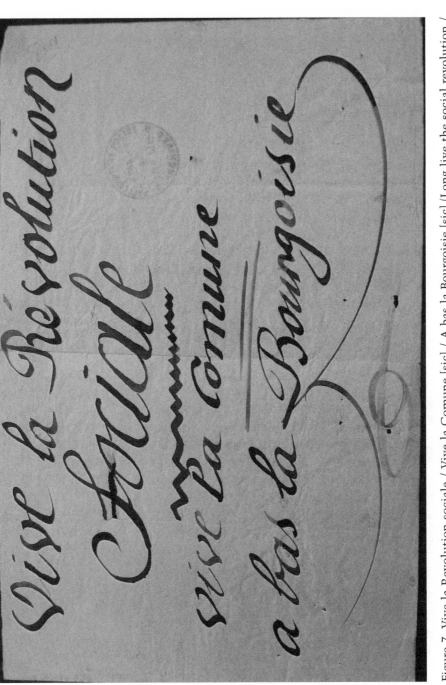

Figure 7. Vive la Revolution sociale / Vive la Commune [sic] / A bas la Bourgoisie [sic] [Long live the social revolution / Long live the Commune / Down with the Bourgeoisie] Hand-painted poster, censored by the Parisian police, Archives de la Préfecture de Police, Paris, BA 478, no. 2363. © Préfecture de Police. All rights reserved.

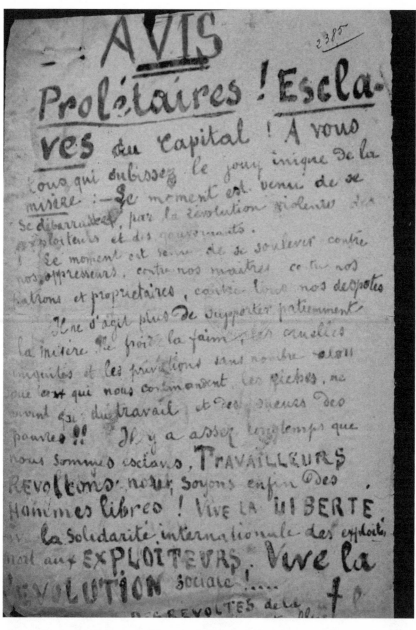

Figure 8. Hand-written anarchist poster ("Avis / Prolétaires! Esclaves du Capital!"), Archives de la Préfecture de Police, Paris, BA 478, no. 2385. © Préfecture de Police. All rights reserved.

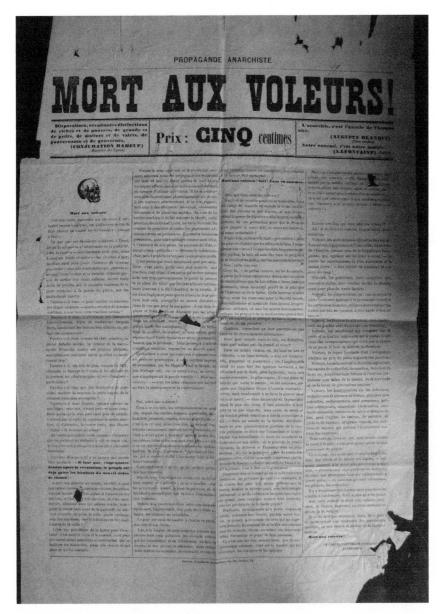

Figure 9. *"Mort aux voleurs !"* (Death to the thieves), censored poster, 1882, Archives de la Préfecture de Police, Paris, BA 472, no. 19. © Préfecture de Police. All rights reserved.

révolutionnaire international, section de France) ended with the slogan "Death to exploiters" ("Mort aux exploiteurs)" (Fig. 10).[58] Both examples encapsulate the inflammatory language often used in manifestos. The "Mort aux exploiteurs" poster was addressed "A vous Bourgeois, Capitalistes, et Gouvernants" and contained a promise of violence and the use of dynamite in the impending class war.[59] The other, addressed to "Esclaves du capital, Travailleurs" contains explicit instructions on how to use dynamite and describes the best way to blow up houses.[60] The daily police reports document a sense of shock that some posters—pasted on walls along rue de Fleuris, rue du Luxembourg, rue Bonaparte, and on the walls of Saint-Sulpice—were found in the more "established" areas of the city and clearly state that these posters were distributed in an attempt to stir up the masses.[61]

As previously noted, political posters of the 1880s and 1890s represented both a physical object around which crowds would gather and a visual stimulus for crowd action. According to Robert Nye, the notion of the "crowd"—as theorized by social psychologists such as Gustave Le Bon and Hippolyte Taine—became increasingly problematic in industrialized nations during these decades. Gustave Le Bon, the leading crowd theorist in fin-de-siècle France, perpetuated and codified this concept of the crowd as potentially dangerous in his landmark work, *Psychologie des foules*. Le Bon defined the "crowd" as a group of people who shared the same collective motivations, emotions, and thoughts for a brief period; a crowd could include religious sects, juries, and parliaments, but Le Bon focused his study on the "criminal crowd" that resorted to mob violence.[62] The

58. BA 472, nos. 21–32 and BA 478, no. 2339–2558.

59. BA 472, no. 25. "We will no longer go down into the street with a hand gun to attack your class that has at its disposal some thousand men armed to the teeth; no, we will only use that which science has revealed to us: chemistry! All devices are suitable for destroying you; from the dagger and dynamite to poison and gasoline. Our socialist theories are supported on science and with its help we will accomplish the socialist liquidation."

60. L. G. "Les Placards à Paris," *Clairon* (Oct. 29,1882), APP BA 478, no. 2389.

61. APP, BA 472, Oct. 1882. The police files (both APP BA 472 and BA 478) from 1882 to 1887 are filled with hundreds of these posters that are torn and stiff with glue.

62. Le Bon, *The Crowd: A Study of the Popular Mind*, 43. "Under certain circumstances, and only under those circumstances, an agglomeration of men presents new characteristics very different from those of individuals composing it. The sentiments and ideas of all the persons in the gathering takes one and the same direction, and their conscious personality vanishes."

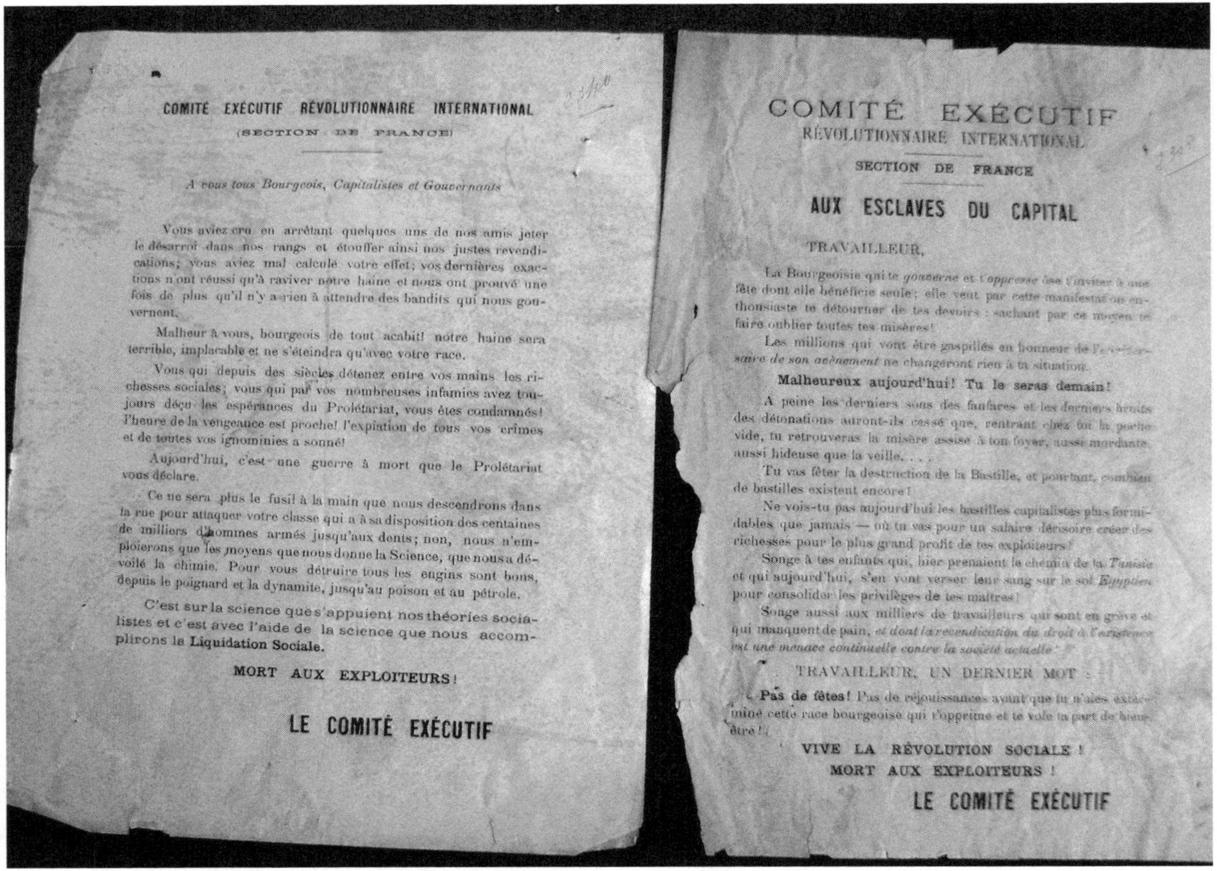

Figure 10. *Comité exécutif révolutionnaire international, section de France*, posters censored by the Parisian Police, c. 1882–1885. Archives de la Préfecture de Police, Paris, BA 478, nos. 2340 and 2306. © Préfecture de Police. All rights reserved.

transformation of individuals into a collective entity in which the will and reasoning of the participants were subjugated occurred only under select conditions in which individuals in a crowd were thought to be held sway by an almost hypnotic force.[63]

In Le Bon's estimation (and his work can be viewed as a summary of ideas that permeated late nineteenth-century thought on the topic), a crowd could be instigated by "exciting causes," stimuli that included the repetition of words or short slogans, such as *liberté* and *égalité*, that produced powerful mental images in the collective mentality of those present.[64] In his opinion, the shouting of political slogans or the display of banners could dramatically affect the behavior of large groups of assembled people. The bold graphics, garish colors, and exaggerated provocative statements of posters, then, are examples of the suggestive slogans described by Le Bon and had been deliberately designed to capture the attention of potential readers and, following Le Bon's line of reasoning, to stimulate crowd action.[65]

This concept of unpredictable crowds was resonant for the censorship of fin-de-siècle political posters. The image of anonymous and purportedly erratic crowds gathering in public streets to discuss the political content of posters signified a type of communal consumption of political propaganda that occurred virtually outside existing institutions and was perceived as threatening for its resistance to regulatory practices.

63. Le Bon, *The Crowd*, 50. Le Bon asserted that the solidification of individuals into a crowd was precipitated by "contagion," "a phenomenon of which it is easy to establish the presence, but that is not easy to explain. It must be classed among those phenomena of the hypnotic order."

64. Le Bon explains the connection between "images"—whether in the form of physical objects, slogans, or simple ideas—and their ability to overwhelm the reasoning capability of the individual within a crowd: "Whatever the ideas suggested to crowds, they can only exercise effective influence on condition that they assume a very absolute, uncompromising, and simple shape. They present themselves then in the guise of images, and are only accessible to the masses under this form. These image-like ideas are not connected by any logical bond of analogy or succession and may take each other's place like the slides of a magic-lantern which the operator withdraws from the groove in which they were placed one above the other." Le Bon, *The Crowd*, 82–83. For an analysis of Le Bon's research as the culmination of crowd psychology in the last decades of the nineteenth century, see Susanna Barrows, *Distorting Mirrors: Visions of the Crowd in Late Nineteenth-Century France* (New Haven and London: Yale University Press, 1981).

65. Political posters either consisted of the front page of a newspaper or, more typically, featured a provocative statement printed in bold, over-sized lettering on brightly colored paper. Unlike their advertising counterparts, political *placards* were rarely illustrated except for the occasional emblem, such as a *fleur-de-lis* or *vanitas* skull.

CONCLUSION

The final effect of the 1881 Press Law and its subsequent revisions in 1882 and 1893–94 was not unfettered press freedom in regards to *affichage*, but rather a more elaborate regulatory system that utilized the Parisian police force to monitor and confiscate material after its distribution. Following over a hundred years in which posters were connected to dissident opinion, the political poster was often cast in a subversive light precisely because it held the promise of directly confronting the masses in a "simultaneous collective experience" that was not "mediated" by church or secular authorities.[66] The censorship of political posters in the 1880s and 1890s depended upon a commonly held association of the poster with working-class insurrection and crowd action that had recently been systematically studied and demonized by social theorists in France. As noted in the reports of the Parisian police force, censorship after 1881 could not be characterized as authoritarian political repression but as a milder, and by consequence, more complicated type of censorship because the Third Republic positioned itself as a government of press freedom while simultaneously monitoring and often subverting the politicization of working-class Parisians.

66. Quoted sections are from Walter Benjamin, "The Work of Art in the Age of Mechanical Reproduction," section XII. (UCLA School of Theater, Film and Television, http:// www.marxist.org /reference/subject/philosophy/works/ge/benjamin.htm [consulted July 21, 2010. Orig. pub. 1936.])

KENNETH GARNER AND RICHARD ABEL

Regulating a Risky Business: Film, Censorship, and Public Safety in Prewar France, 1909–1914

In the summer of 1912, the French film industry found itself facing its gravest political crisis of the pre-World War I era. Responding to publicized concerns that crime films were contributing to a widely perceived escalating wave of juvenile violence, the mayors of several major provincial towns, including Lyon and Marseille, passed municipal ordinances (*arrêtés municipaux*) blocking the exhibition of such pictures and ordering that theater owners who showed them be arrested. Under such headlines as "Declaration of War on the Cinema" and "The Cinema's Liberty Is In Peril," the French cinema press, spearheaded by George Dureau's *Ciné-journal*, took the lead in responding to what they perceived was not only the arbitrary imposition of municipal power but also the unfair singling-out of the film industry for producing material that was, after all, comparable to "legitimate" theaters, *café-concerts*, crime novels, and the popular press. If crime films were to be censored, Dureau rhetorically asked, why not prohibit, for instance, "scandalous scenes that injure all men of good taste in the numerous *café-concerts* [in Paris]?"[1]

This perception of unfairness in the 1912–13 censorship debate was part of the industry's broader dialogue with the Republican state over its relationship to the French public. Central to this dialogue was the notion of "public safety" and the perception, at least among municipal authorities, that the film industry posed particular risks. Broadly speaking, the Republican state defined the industry's threat to public safety as both moral and physical: criminal films, often de-

1. Georges Dureau, "Paris ne suivra pas l'exemple des Maires de Province!" *Ciné-journal* (CJ) 209 (24 August 1912): 4. Translations throughout are by the authors unless otherwise noted.

YFS 122, *Out of Sight: Political Censorship of the Visual Arts in Nineteenth-Century France*, ed. Goldstein, © 2012 by Yale University.

scribed as pornographic, would corrupt impressionable youth and lead to their demoralization. The related fears of "pornography," juvenile crime, and moral dissolution open up a window onto the anxieties of the French Third Republic—the perception of rising crime, urbanization, and industrialization. The crisis over film censorship also reveals the contradictory orientation of Republican politics as outlined by Pierre Rosanvallon: on the one hand, aiming to establish a secular society rooted in the defense of civil liberties and male suffrage; on the other, channeling the local and regional political activities of associations to enhance the regulatory power of the state.[2] As studies on development have shown, states often pursue ameliorative policies as a means to extend their administrative power.[3] With rising fears of both random juvenile violence and the growth of working-class militancy, moderate Republicans and moral leagues advocated for state regulation of cinemas in defense of public morality.[4] While private associations like the moral leagues formed the bedrock of political activity, their ultimate effect was "to widen the traditional sphere of the State."[5]

Our essay thus argues that the emergence of French film censorship can only be understood as part of a broader effort by the Republican state to extend its regulatory power in the name of public safety. The controversy over theater closings led to the first of a series of progressively centralized controls over film content and exhibition practices. These controls had their origins in legislation related to the theater and other public performances that stretched back to the French Revolution. However, film presented a particular problem for

---

2. Pierre Rosanvallon, *Le modèle politique français: la société civile contre le jacobinisme de 1789 à nos jours* (Paris: Éditions du Seuil, 2004).

3. See Michel Foucault, *Discipline and Punish: The Birth of Prison*, trans. Alan Sheridan (New York: Random House, 1975) and Alain Corbin, *Les filles de noce: misère sexuelle et prostitution (19e siècle)* (Paris: Flammarion, 1982), esp. 474–80. On development and state administrative power, see Paul Rabinow, *French Modern: Norms and Forms of the Social Environment* (Cambridge, MA: MIT, 1989); Timothy Mitchell, *Rule of Experts: Egypt, Techno-Politics, Modernity* (Berkeley, CA: University of California, 2001); and Chandra Mukerji, *Impossible Engineering: Technology and Territoriality on the Canal du Midi* (Princeton, NJ: Princeton University Press, 2009).

4. Sanford Elwitt, *The Third Republic Defended: Bourgeois Reform in France, 1880–1914* (Baton Rouge, LA: Louisiana State University Press, 1986); Judith Stone. *The Search for Social Peace: Reform Legislation in France 1890–1914* (Albany, NY: SUNY Press, 1985); and Jean-Marie Mayer, *La vie politique sous la Troisième République 1870–1940* (Paris: Éditions du Seuil, 1984), 161–67.

5. Rosanvallon, 393.

those who would regulate as well as defend it—was it a new form of dramatic theater, a new kind of public spectacle (*spectacles de curiosité*), or something that encompassed, yet differed, from both? And, consequently, who was capable of judging the morality of films shown to a wide diversity of audiences? In order to understand how film censorship emerged in the pre-World War I era, we need both to understand the political culture of the Third Republic and to evoke the anxieties that troubled its sense of social order.

SPECTACLES AND THE LAW: AN OVERVIEW

Many scholars have ably traced the history behind French film censorship.[6] As both scholars of French cinema and historians of cultural censorship have shown, film censorship had its origins in government concerns over theaters and other forms of popular spectacle.[7] Although written texts had been the concern of censors since the Ancien Régime and the Enlightenment, "they feared even more the potential impact of *visual* and *aural* expression, such as that offered by caricature, theater, opera, songs, and cinema."[8] Given the difficulty that French governments had in sustaining legitimacy during the nineteenth century—between 1815 and 1914 France had two monarchies (Bourbon, Orléanist), two republics (the second and the third), and a restored Bonapartist empire—public authorities were especially concerned that popular spectacles were a subversive sphere that could potentially incite social, especially lower class, unrest. Although the Third Republic that gradually solidified its power during the 1870s did so, in part, because it successfully used popular festivals and spectacles to inculcate Republican values, nonetheless, "it also maintained theater and caricature censorship and continued to pros-

6. See Robert Justin Goldstein, *The War for the Public Mind: Political Censorship in Nineteenth-Century Europe* (Westport, CT: Praeger, 2000), 125–173; Goldstein, *Political Censorship of the Arts and Press in Nineteenth-Century Europe* (New York: St. Martin's Press, 1989), 175–82; Alain Montaigne, *Histoire juridique des interdits cinématographiques en France (1909–2001)* (Paris: L'Harmattan, 2007), 19–28; Richard Abel, *The Ciné Goes to Town, French Cinema 1896–1914* (Berkeley, CA: University of California, 1994), ch. 1; Paul Leglise, *La politique du cinéma français: le cinéma et la IIIème République* (Paris: L'Herminier, 1970), 25–33; and Neville March Hemmings, *Film Censors and the Law*, (London: George Allen & Unwin, 1967), 332–360.

7. See Goldstein, "The Debate over Censorship of Caricature in Nineteenth-Century France," *Art Journal* 48/1 (Spring, 1989): 9–15.

8. Goldstein, *The War for the Public Mind*, 127.

ecute the written press."[9] As the Republic secured a firmer foothold, controls of the written press were increasingly relaxed—especially after the Press Law of 29 July 1881—yet censorship of the theater would persist until 1906.

The more stringent controls over theaters and the constant surveillance of such popular spectacles as *café-concerts* and popular theaters indicate that authorities focused on two kinds of subversion: criticisms of the ruling governments and public authorities, and a more general concern over the circulation of such licentious and "immoral" ideas as sexual freedom, Paul Lafargue's "the right to be lazy," and criminality that threatened to erode the bases upon which a sound social and moral order could be established.[10] Although censors prohibited filmmakers from treating certain political subjects like the Dreyfus Affair, as we will see, they were far more concerned about the morally corrupting impact of the cinema than its potential for political subversion.

Nonetheless, what is important to note is that censorship of cinema did not suddenly "spring up" as a result of the proliferation of "criminal films" in the 1909–1912 period, but had its roots in the regulation and surveillance of popular spectacle whose legal basis extended back to the French Revolution, when the Constituent Assembly passed a law regulating public spectacles in August of 1790. This law subjected public spectacles to the authority of municipal officials, although, at this point, the law exempted legitimate theaters. Theatrical censorship waxed and waned throughout the nineteenth century, alternating between periods of tight control, such as during

9. Goldstein, *The War for the Public Mind*, 156. Scholars who have looked at the Republic's efforts to ground its values through popular spectacle and the creation of public festivities include Charles Rearick, *Pleasures of the Belle Époque: Entertainment and Festivity in Turn-of-the-Century France* (New Haven, CT: Yale University Press, 1985); James Lehning, *To Be a Citizen: The Political Culture of the Early Third Republic* (Ithaca, N.Y.: Cornell University Press, 2001); Lehning, *The Melodramatic Thread: Spectacle and Political Culture in Modern France* (Bloomington, IN: Indiana University Press, 2007). Historians have also given more attention to the efforts of the Second Empire to inculcate Bonapartism and specifically a cult of personality around Napoleon III. See Matthew Truesdell, *Spectacular politics: Louis-Napoleon Bonaparte and the Fête impériale, 1849–1870* (Oxford: Oxford University Press, 1997) and Sudhir Hazareesingh, *The Saint-Napoleon: Celebrations of Sovereignty in Nineteenth-Century France* (Cambridge, MA: Harvard University Press, 2004).

10. See Goldstein, *Political Censorship*, 113–54; for Lafargue, see Rearick, *Pleasures of the Belle Epoque*, ch. 2.

the Napoleonic and Restoration eras and its firm resumption by the July Monarchy in 1835 despite an initial relaxation in the immediate aftermath of the 1830 Revolution.[11] During its liberal phase, the Second Empire passed a law (1864) requiring that theatrical performances obtain prior authorization from the Minister of Beaux-Arts and, in the provinces, by departmental prefects. The Republic retained theatrical censorship and vigorously suppressed productions that made reference to the Commune during the 1870s.[12] Nonetheless, as the Republic became more secure, surveillance of legitimate theaters became so lax that the Legislature effectively abolished theatrical censorship by refusing to allocate funds in the Finance Law of 1906.[13] Public spectacles, by contrast, ultimately received the classification of *spectacles de curiosité* and consisted of "marionettes, *cafés chantants, cafés concerts* and other establishments of the same kind," which remained firmly under the control of municipalities and, more specifically, of mayors.[14]

The Third Republic reaffirmed the mayors' authority over *spectacles de curiosité*. This was undoubtedly due to the greater potential for such popular entertainments to foster political or moral subversion among the "laboring classes, dangerous classes." The Municipal Law of 5 April 1884 asserted his responsibility for maintaining public order, his authority over the municipal police, and his power over public spectacles. The law was designed to devolve certain responsibilities to the localities in an effort toward greater decentralization, while at the same time more effectively aligning the municipalities with the political prerogatives of the Republican state: "between local power and the surveillance and tutorial function of the State."[15] Composed of middle-class professionals (*les nouvelles couches sociales*), the post-1879 Republic set about cementing such Republican objectives as *laïcité*, equal suffrage (for adult men), and civil liberties within a parliamentary regime topped by a weak executive. Its durability rested in its heterogeneity and in its efforts in fostering social cohesion: Republicanism was itself a flexible enough ideology to accommodate a diverse array of social groups including small shopkeepers, businessmen, academics, and even some sections of the working

---

11. Goldstein, *Political Censorship*, 116–17.
12. Goldstein, *Political Censorship*, 138.
13. Leglise, 27–29.
14. Hemmings, 332.
15. Rosanvallon, 361.

class.[16] Yet as Rosanvallon and other scholars have recently noted, the Third Republic increasingly found itself caught between Republican ideals of *liberté, egalité, fraternité* and the state's desire to act as tutelary power over French society, regulating public life and restricting civil associations, labor unions, and any other potential threats to the creation of a stable Republican polity.[17] "The dissociation of the social and the political," Rosanvallon writes, "is at the heart of the reformed Republican model such as it was put in place during the 1880–1914 period."[18]

Consequently, laws like the 1884 Municipal Law contained both the ideological aspirations of Republicanism, promoting decentralization through the affirmation of local authority, while simultaneously augmenting the state's tutelary and regulatory presence in social life. Such decentralization that did occur, then, was mainly instrumental, "strictly on the order of personnel [*gestion*] and not concerned with the functioning of public powers."[19] Mayors' policing powers in their localities were thus clarified and strengthened, but at the same time they themselves were now compelled to monitor spectacles more closely for any potential threats to the emerging Republican social and moral order. Should they refuse to ban a spectacle deemed a threat by the state-appointed prefect, the Municipal Law allowed the prefect to override the mayor and ban it himself. Because prefects were the chief administrators of *départements* and appointed by the French state, they legally could overrule mayors, who were elected by local constituencies, although generally they maintained an outward respect for the latter's prerogative. A contemporary commentator underscored this tension between local authority and state compulsion: "with regard to spectacle establishments, the mayor has the right and *the duty* to keep watch in the name of public order and notably to *forbid* or close down productions capable of troubling it."[20]

Motion pictures were screened publicly for the first time a decade after the Municipal Law was passed and thus had no initial legal classification. Initially, most subjects were quite short: *actualités*, scenes

16. See Michel Winock, *La Belle Époque: La France de 1900 à 1914* (Paris: Perrin, 2003), 21–23.

17. See, for example, Lehning (2001).

18. Rosanvallon, 355.

19. Rosanvallon, 363.

20. M. Grelot, quoted in René Bérenger. *Manuel pratique pour la lutte contre la pornographie* (Paris: Imprimerie Mouillot, 1907), 79.

from daily life, historical re-enactments, comic variety turns, dances, and magic acts. Although motion pictures appeared as one of many performances on music hall and *café-concert* programs in large cities, they were shown principally in fairground cinemas within the regular circuits of popular traveling *fêtes foraines*.[21] Consequently, they were widely considered to be *spectacles de curiosité* rather than legitimate theater and did not benefit from the repeal of theatrical censorship in June 1906, which prompted Pathé later that year to begin opening a chain of permanent urban cinemas. Indeed, it was Pathé's production of a controversial *actualité* that led to the first governmental intervention in 1909 and ultimately to the crisis of 1912. In order to understand why an *actualité* would lead to the creation of film censorship, we need to explore the underlying anxieties of Republican France.

PUBLIC SAFETY AND THE MORAL ORDER: LE DESTIN FABULEUX DE RENÉ BÉRENGER

While mayoral and prefectural power over spectacles shows the extent to which the Republican state sought to extend its regulatory power in social life, it is no less the case that *fin-de-siècle* Frenchmen perceived their increasingly urbanized and industrialized world with increasing anxiety. Their fears encompassed many features of urban modernity—rising crime, prostitution, violent accidents on tramways and subways—all stoked by the popular press.[22] By 1911, for example, Paris's population had reached nearly three million people while its immediate suburbs (*banlieues*) expanded to accommodate the nation's rising industrial work force and an influx of immigrants from southern Europe.[23] The urban-industrial concentration around

21. Abel, *The Ciné Goes to Town*, 16, 24. Advertisements for early motion pictures chiefly appeared in the trade journal, *L'industriel foraine*.

22. For crime, see Robert A. Nye. *Crime, Madness and Politics in Modern France: The Medical Concept of National Decline* (Princeton, 1984); on prostitution, see Corbin, 1992. Anxieties over the destructive power of new technologies and urban life have been recently analyzed by Bernhard Rieger, *Technology and the Culture of Modernity in Britain and Germany, 1890–1945* (Cambridge, 2005), and Peter S. Soppelsa, *The Fragility of Modernity: Infrastructure and Everyday Life in Paris, 1870–1914* (Ph.D. dissertation, University of Michigan, 2009). For the sensationalist press, see Gregory K. Shaya, *Mayhem for Moderns.* (Ph.D. dissertation, University of Michigan, 2000).

23. Winock, 69. For the *banlieues*, see Jean Bastié, *La croissance de la banlieue parisienne* (Paris: Presses Universitaires de France, 1964) and Tyler Stovall, *The Rise of the Paris Red Belt* (Berkeley, CA: University of California,1990).

Paris and France's other major cities prompted reformers, newspapermen, and medical specialists to decry what they perceived to be a rising incidence of crime and immorality. They focused especially on crimes involving young people—prostitution and the white slave trade as well as assaults and murders by "Apaches," gangs of young men (often foreigners) from Paris's suburbs and "*bandes à Bonnot*," (automobile thieves), named after their leading practitioner—Jules Bonnot—whose dramatic death during a gun fight with police would provide the cinematic fodder that would precipitate the 1912 crisis. Although actual crime rates remained relatively stable in the pre-World War I period, popular perception of rising crime expressed latent anxieties about modernity and made public safety an important topic in the press and in political debate.[24] As Judith Stone has argued, "security . . . was the central objective which drew all sectors of the bourgeoisie together . . . . All agreed that their security could be jeopardized by the new conditions of an industrializing society and the new, militant demands of an enfranchised working class."[25]

The powerful senator René Bérenger (1830–1915) was one of the principal proponents for moral reform legislation and a key advocate for the surveillance and censorship of public spectacles.[26] Originally from the Drôme region, he worked as an *avocat général* (assistant public prosecutor) in Grenoble and Lyon before being elected to the Senate in 1875. Though a committed Republican, he was also a devout Catholic who believed that, while the Church should have no influence over public affairs, "the state would lose its sense of duty if it failed to grant not only its protection but also its favor to those with religious convictions."[27] While his early senatorial efforts focused on prison reform, by the mid-1890s Bérenger had committed himself wholeheartedly to the fight against prostitution and public displays of immorality. What is noteworthy in Bérenger's argument is that the latter necessarily produces the former—that illicit images corrupt the sensibilities of young people, especially girls. Arguing for his proposition for a law on prostitution in April 1894, which would ultimately

---

24. Winock, 176.

25. Stone, 23.

26. For a summary biography, see Annie Lamarre, "René Bérenger," in *Les immortels du Sénat 1875–1918: Les cent seize inamovibles de la Troisième République*, ed. J.M. Mayeur and A. Corbin (Paris: Publications de la Sorbonne, 1995), 222–25.

27. Mayeur and Corbin, 223.

fail, Bérenger's main goal was "to 'purge' the street and the public spaces, to fight against the teaching through the eyes (*l'enseignment par les yeux*) of immorality."[28]

Bérenger's efforts privileged more popular cultural and image-oriented displays of "immorality" than literary ones. His *Manuel pratique pour la lutte contre la pornographie* (1907) claims not only that "the press and, in particular, the illustrated journal . . . is one of many agents of demoralization" but also, in referring to the 1882 Anti-obscenity Law, so are "writings, printings other than books, posters, drawings, engravings, paintings, emblems and obscene images."[29] To show was to inculcate. Indeed, for Bérenger and his acolytes, immorality was inherently a public spectacle—it necessitated not only that something be *seen* but that it be *viewable* in a public space. The leader of the Ligue Marseillaise pour la défense de la moralité, who called the senator the "inspiration of our League," defined pornography as that "featured in book-store windows, and in kiosks in train stations. A lucrative, flourishing industry that pleases by exhibiting all the temptations of lust, the desires of the flesh, and that attracts a crowd of spectators."[30]

The theater, however, embodied the gravest moral threat. Here Bérenger went beyond a concern for the actual *content* of a specific production. Rather, what was most corrupting, in his view, was the overall experience of the performance. The theater "speaks directly to the senses. The arrangement of the hall, the *mise-en-scène*, the lighting, the music, the costumes, as well as the unfolding action and the performances of the actors, collude to give greater force to the physical sensation and to fix it in the memory."[31] Consequently, the theater heightened one's sensual appreciation and rendered one more susceptible to immoral influences so that, as Bérenger's Marseillais acolyte put it, spectators "listen to and applaud in our principal theaters the most proscribed dialogues, the most daring and raciest scenes."[32]

---

28. Corbin, 463.
29. Bérenger, 68, 117.
30. Speech by M.E. Delibes, president of the *Ligue marseillaise pour la défense la moralité publique: Assemblée générale tenue le 26 avril 1904, au palais de justice* (Marseille: Barlatier, 1904), 7–8.
31. Bérenger, 74.
32. Delibes, 8.

To combat this pervasive indecency, in 1894 Bérenger founded the Ligue pour la lutte contre la licence des rues (eventually renamed the Société centrale de protestation contre la licence des rues). He became quite active in promoting the creation of provincial societies, as the Marseille League's president attests. In March 1905, representatives from over fifty of these societies met in Bordeaux to create a national Fédération des sociétés contre la pornographie with Bérenger as its president. These leagues, it must be stressed, were secular organizations and not organized or directed by Church authorities. Their leadership included mayors, professors, and journal editors but not members of the clergy. Consequently, the leagues embodied the contradictions in French Republicanism—on the one hand, they were organized to allow their members to engage in and put pressure on local and municipal politics, and yet their ultimate objective was to extend the reach of the regulatory state. Bérenger's *Manuel pratique* reproduces the program that came out of the Fédération's organization meeting in Bordeaux; one of their requests is "that the Minister of the Interior invite the municipalities to retract [*subordonner*] the concessions or authorizations that they give to kiosks and generally to display windows on public streets and to restrict the display and the sale of books, images, postcards, and obscene publications."[33]

By 1905, Bérenger presided over a powerful network of associations that, based on the strategies described in the *Manuel pratique*, knew how to pressure local authorities, disrupt public spectacles, start letter campaigns, and organize public protests. They appear to have targeted theatrical performances with considerable vigor. The manual mentions that the leagues were able to get municipal authorities to ban six plays outright between 1900 and 1907. A court case in Lyon revealed how the League exerted pressure on theater owners. First, they would send letters to theater owners warning them that "if they persist in this exhibition, the League would find itself obliged to lodge a complaint" with the municipal authorities.[34] Should the threat of official sanction fail, the Leagues would then place posters near the offending theaters as a way of rallying public protests. In the Lyon case, a theater owner—one M. Martini—failed to win his suit against the Ligue pour le relèvement de la moralité publique, when he

33. Bérenger, 159.
34. Bérenger, 144.

argued that such protests had reduced the turnout for two of his productions, *La bonne à tout faire* and *La casserole*. The Lyonnais civil tribunal ruled that the public had the right to express opprobrium and displeasure about theatrical performances and that "each person is free to judge and to censure plays, provided that the critiques produced be exempt from bad faith and are disinterested."[35] That the collective action of an association was considered by legal authorities to be the equivalent of an individual person's critique and judgment was due to the 1901 Law of Associations, which legally recognized associations (excepting congregations and labor unions) for the first time. According to this law, the association was "a contract, nothing more, nothing less" between private individuals, and was "an instrument of individualism, not a form of communitarianism. . . . It belonged completely to the private sphere and in no way interfered with the public sphere."[36] The League's belligerent pressure on spectacles and theaters was thus accepted and protected, in the eyes of the state, as a form of free speech articulated by private individuals. "To decide otherwise," the Lyonnais tribunal concluded, "would be to admit to the negation of all critique. This is impossible in a society like ours, founded on the liberty of thought and the free discussion of ideas."[37]

Despite the official abrogation of theatrical censorship in June 1906, therefore, legitimate theaters and public spectacles were under the scrutinizing gaze of municipal officials and moral associations, both of whom saw them as threats to the public order and both of whom sought either directly or indirectly to extend the Republican state's regulatory reach. Although cinema escaped official classification as either legitimate theater or *spectacle de curiosité*, it was regarded by moralists like Bérenger and public officials in the same light. In a 1910 editorial, *Ciné-journal*'s editor Georges Dureau sniffed that "the pre-conceived idea of M. Bérenger, who has been called Father Shame [*Père-le-Pudeur*] in the past for good reason, is that the cinema is a school of vice in the service of juvenile crime." He went on to explain that "the starting point of his [Bérenger's] moralizing campaign is that all theatrical spectacles are bad because the many modes of representing life according to its appearances are too close

35. Bérenger, 130.
36. Rosanvallon, 328.
37. Bérenger, 130–131.

to reality. This strange disdainer of art . . . does not wish to give to cinema the privilege that is usually conceded to the theater . . . [that the] cinema [is] a moralizer and educator . . . [and] one of the forms of modern dramatic art."[38] Yet, ironically, it was not cinema's similarity to theatrical drama but rather to the *spectacles de curosité* that provoked the censorship crisis in the immediate prewar period.

SPECTACULAR *ACTUALITÉS* AND CINEMATIC CRIMES

Cinema emerged in a social world defined by increasing concern over the consequences of urban modernity and, consequently, it shared much of the same criticism that was leveled against other popular spectacles – namely, that it had the potential to erode public morality.[39] This did not mean, however, that the cinema's political import was ignored. As Robert Goldstein has noted, "all films dealing with the Dreyfus Affair were banned after a documentary on the subject touched off riots in 1899," and as "international tensions increased on the eve of World War I, in 1913 local officials were urged to ban all portrayals of characters appearing in German uniform."[40] Since early French filmmakers stayed away from overtly political subjects, critics like Bérenger and others concentrated on the cinema's threat to the Republic's *moral* order. Although the governments of most European countries expressed similar concerns at this time, in France the debate seems to have become particularly acute in the prewar period given the emergence of the popular genre of crime films and a widely-perceived (though unfounded) concomitant rise of juvenile crime.[41] Although they reached their apogee only later with the *Fantômas* and *Les vampires* series of the 1913–1916 era, prewar crime films were still very popular, despite their consisting mainly of re-enactments of celebrated crimes and different types of executions. Many of these films featured representations of "Apaches," bands of young males from Paris's booming suburbs to whom the press and the public

38. George Dureau, "Le Sénateur Bérenger contre le cinématographe," *CJ* 3/109, 24 September 1910, 3.
39. See Ben Singer's *Melodrama and Modernity* (New York, NY: Columbia University Press, 2001) for an analysis of film melodrama's articulation of urban fears and anxieties in the USA.
40. Goldstein, *The War for the Public Mind*, 158.
41. For other European countries' responses to cinematic immorality, see Goldstein (1989), 177–82.

attributed the rise in violent, juvenile criminality. Re-enactments of crimes and especially of executions became a popular, if disreputable, sub-genre—a staged *actualité*—which provoked the annoyance of public authorities and respectable critical opinion. "Apache" crimes were a mainstay of the popular press in *fin-de-siècle* France and both sociologists and journalists published tracts on their origins, culture, and criminal acts.[42] Bérenger himself had sponsored an 1898 criminal law that allowed the police to prosecute underage offenders. Within the first four years after its passage, over 1,300 youths were brought in front of tribunals, although the majority of these were ultimately acquitted.[43] Nevertheless, and especially in the 1907–1910 period, the popular press continued to fan widespread anxieties over "Apaches" and "bandes à Bonnot" leading authorities such as Georges Clemenceau, then Minister of the Interior, to enact reforms of the police force and the Legislature to reinstitute the death penalty for capital crimes, which had fallen into abeyance, in December 1908. The first victims of the new law were four criminals who were executed simultaneously in Béthune in January 1909.

Although the Ministry of Justice issued a circular prohibiting any filming of the execution, a skillful Pathé cameraman managed to capture it, and the company promptly released *La quadruple exécution capitale de Béthune* (1909). This provoked an immediate response from Clemenceau's Interior Ministry, which issued a circular to prefects banning all public showings of execution genre films and declaring that cinematic spectacles "did not belong with the representation of dramatic works, in the sense of the law, but rather in the category of *spectacles de curiosité*."[44] As scholars have repeatedly pointed out, this ministerial circular marks the first decisive step in the creation of a film censorship regime: for the first time, an official government agency classified films as *spectacles de curiosité* and thereby arrogated to mayors and, by extension, prefects the power over their exhibition. But a ministerial circular was not an act of law and consequently legal jurisdiction over film exhibition remained unclear. "In 1909," one scholar states unequivocally, "no legislative text and no juridical act specified the cinema as a *spectacle de curiosité*."[45]

42. Winock, 178–82.

43. Jacques Bourquin, "René Bérenger et la loi de 1898," *Revue histoire d'enfance irrégulière* 2 (1999). See http://rhei.revues.org/document31.html

44. Montagne, 23.

45. Montagne, 24.

What *was* cinema, then? "One of the forms of modern dramatic art" or a public spectacle? Was it more like theatrical productions where municipal intervention would only occur at the behest of pressure groups like Bérenger's and his acolytes' leagues? Or was it such a threat to public safety that state intervention and regulation were necessary? And who had the ultimate authority to regulate its exhibition—mayors of municipalities or prefects? The cinema press, especially Dureau's *Ciné-journal*, argued that cinema was a form of dramatic art and like the legitimate theater, its purpose was to move and edify audiences, not instruct them. "In itself," Dureau argued, "the cinematographic film is only a theatrical expression of life; it must be judged as independent from all other [artistic] forms because it is moral, not scientific. . . . More simply, let us say that films must, in order to achieve their goal, make us *laugh* or *move* us."[46] Consequently, the idea that even a young person would be corrupted by witnessing a criminal act was absurd—would one say the same thing of audiences attending classical tragedy? "There are classical tragedies filled with such 'criminal acts,'" another editor complained, "and I don't know whether Senator Béranger [sic] himself would rise up against 'Oedipus Rex' or 'Iphigenia.'"[47]

Indeed, the cinema press occasionally pushed this argument further, making a virtue out of cinema's ambiguous legal status. Cinema was both theater *and* spectacle—and because it attracted all types of spectators, including women and children, it could not afford to alienate them by exhibiting licentious material. "Can one suppose that [exhibitors] would consciously commit the error of giving the essentially neutral public condemnable pleasures or emotions?" Dureau asked. "This would mean believing that they are capable of suicide, since inevitably their theaters would be promptly closed or deserted."[48] Obscene films were, consequently, an anomaly made by clandestine producers outside of the "legitimate" business and exhibited only in disreputable places.[49] The official industry was all sweetness and light—combining the mass appeal of the public spectacle with the emotional affect of the theater. Dureau, in yet another

46. Georges Dureau, "La cinématographie est une oeuvre d'art: elle n'est au service exclusive ni de la morale ni de l'enseignement," *CJ* 4/160 (16 September 1911) : 3–4.

47. F. Laurent, "La tragédie au cinéma," *Le cinéma* 1/17 (21 June 1912) : 1.

48. Dureau, "Le cinématographe est-il une école de corruption?" *CJ* 2/55 (6–12 September 1909) : 1.

49. R. Rialc, "Les films obscènes," *Le cinéma* (15 March 1912) : 1.

editorial, gushed that "[our industry] knows how to amuse the whole world by the innocence of its laughter and the amusing actions of its first rank artists . . ." and concluded that "it is today the general theater of the people."[50]

Nonetheless, *Ciné-journal* leaves the definite impression that, in the years before the 1912 crisis, the industry felt increasing pressure from the moralistic associations and public authorities. "At this moment in all countries, and even in France," Dureau wrote in mid-1911, "the most shameless spirits [*les esprits les moins pudibonds*] are leading serious, and decidedly invasive, campaigns against pornography, and I think that cinema producers must redouble their prudence in the choice of films offered to the public."[51] Later that summer, Dureau reported that Bérenger's Société central de protestation contre la licence des rues "had circulated a petition demanding a more energetic intervention by public authorities against pornography" listing *cinématographes* as "one of the great dangers at this time."[52] Dureau again cautioned prudence: "the cinema avoids pornography. . . . Let's maintain this position and . . . leave to the music hall, to the *café-concert*, to the cabaret and the small theaters the dangerous monopoly on licentiousness."[53] Yet, it seems clear that both moral associations and even the Church were stepping up their pressure on municipal authorities for greater intervention. *Ciné-journal* reprinted a communiqué from the Archbishop of Lyon fretting that, "a certain number of fathers and mothers had been alarmed" at what was being shown at their local cinemas: "it is not rare, in effect, that the program reserved for children features scenes of *Apaches* robbing passers-by, breaking into houses, assassinating their owners, or contains scenes of domestic quarrels . . . which often end in murder or suicide."[54] At the same time the Parisian Ligue contre la licence published a tract encouraging its colleagues in the provinces to "act using all means—legal procedures (*démarches*), the press, protests, petitions, posters, (*constats d'huisser*)—upon the *mayor*, who has all the necessary powers to forbid and even suspend immoral productions."[55]

50. Dureau, "Défendons notre industrie!" *CJ* 5/187 (28 March 1912) : 3.
51. Dureau, "De la moralité des films," *CJ* 4/147 (17 June 1911) : 3.
52. Dureau, "Surveillons nos programmes!" *CJ* 4/150 (8 July 1911) : 6.
53. Ibid, 7.
54. "Surveillons nos programmes," *CJ* 4/148 (24 June 1911) : 15.
55. Ibid., 16.

The debate even reached the floor of the Senate in late 1911 when the conservative Lyonnais senator, Paul Cazeneuve, sought to include cinema within the 1882 Anti-obscenity Law that set fines and jail sentences for those committing "offense to public morals" (a separate law from the 1884 Municipal Law that allowed mayors to close down public spectacles). Cazeneuve's rationale is noteworthy because, like Bérenger's on the theater, it defines cinema's corruptibility less in terms of specific content than the sensory interaction with the medium itself:

> I will say that, on the influence it exercises on spectators, there is an incontestable danger in the animation of scenes, as a result of movement. The animated image has a suggestive influence that no one can misunderstand and is as pernicious as it is immoral. . . . If you examine closely a band of celluloid, you will not see obscene images; it is only a series of small drawings destined to succeed each other very rapidly to produce the desired effect by the unrolling of the film.[56]

The debate over cinema's "immorality" ultimately compelled both public authorities and those within the industry to speculate on the nature of cinema—a form of theater, a public spectacle, a series of photograms, a projection of moving images. It seems clear, however, that all sides were being pushed into this debate by the moral associations and conservative figures like Bérenger and Cazeneuve, who used anxieties over crime and its cinema representation to lobby for greater state regulation. By December 1911, they seemed to have achieved the upper hand, as Dureau wearily noted,

> The film industry is more and more under surveillance by our zealously anti-pornographic, moralizing magistrates. I will not stop from repeating . . . that the public authorities are watching for an occasion to impose restrictive rules on us, in the name of the outraged prudery of I don't know which spectators.[57]

He wouldn't have to wait long.

THE CRISIS OF 1912 AND THE ORIGINS OF FRENCH FILM CENSORSHIP

When the mayors of several provincial cities and towns decided to restrict public exhibition of crime films and, in a few cases, prosecute theater owners, their actions were less arbitrary than they might at

---

56. "La cinématographie devant le Sénat," *CJ* 4/171 (2 December 1911) : 13–14.
57. Ibid., 13.

first appear. Pressured by the moral leagues, provoked by concerns over public safety, and seemingly endowed with the power over cinema as a form of *spectacle de curiosité* (although only a ministerial circular had placed cinema in this category), they decided to exercise their authority against theaters that showed films. The first interdiction occurred in the small town of Belley (Ain) in early June, when the mayor forbade the showing of two films, *Bandits en automobile* and *Hors la loi*, purporting to show the April, 1912, police raid that killed the armed robber, Jules Bonnot. His action was strongly supported by the Parisian daily, *Le temps*, which contended that such crime films actually served as a form of propaganda and cultural validation for "Apaches" and *bandes à Bonnot*: "It's with a certain pride that 'Apaches' see in the newspapers and in film the portrait and the exploits of their comrades."[58] The industry almost immediately suffered a more devastating hit when Édouard Herriot, the mayor of Lyon and rising star on the Republican Radical left, also forbade all screenings of films representing criminal acts on June 14.

It was one thing for "Père-le-Pudeur" Bérenger and the mayor of a small town to come out against the cinema, quite another to have the mayor of France's second largest city, and a prominent national politician to follow suit. Whereas Dureau's response to the mayor of Belley's interdiction was measured and even a little condescending, Herriot's actions clearly shocked him. In an open letter to Herriot, Dureau appealed to his political convictions, his defense of the freedom of the press, and his considerable cultural background to ask why cinema should be singled out.[59] What did prompt Herriot? Although neither of his recent biographers nor his memoirs ever discuss this incident, it seems likely that he was responding to pressure from the moral leagues.[60] Lyon was the only city with two active moral leagues—the Ligue lyonnaise contre l'immoralité de la rue, and the Ligue française pour le relèvement de la moralité—the latter of which was described by Bérenger as "one of the most active of our societies," and whose "zealous" leader, M. Hemmel, served on the

58. Reprinted in Dureau, "Le cinéma tel que le juge la grande presse française," *CJ* 5/199 (15 June 1912) : 3.

59. Dureau, "Lettre ouverte à M. Herriot, maire de Lyon et à ses imitateurs," *CJ* 5/201 (29 June 1912) : 3–5.

60. Gérard Chauv, *Edouard Herriot (1872–1957) et le radicalisme triomphant* (Lyon: LUGD, 1996); Louis Muron, *Eduoard Herriot (1872–1957)* (Lyon: Éditions Lyonnaises d'Art et d'Histoire, 1997); and Eduoard Herriot, *Jadis*, Vol 1. (Paris: Flammarion, 1948).

executive committee for Bérenger's Fédération des societies contre la pornographie. It was Hemmel's group that pressured theater owners like M. Martini and was also effective in organizing public protests at offending productions.[61]

Nonetheless, Herriot's action seems to have opened the flood-gates. By August mayors had issued decrees (arrêtés) in Hyères (Var), Bordeaux, Marseille, Lille, Rouen, Montpelier, and Aix-en-Provence; elsewhere, mayors required all films to be submitted for municipal review before exhibition.[62] Taken aback, the cinema press's defense of the film industry shifted away from its similarity to the dramatic theater and toward an emphasis on its photographic and documentary aspect. Dureau chastised the mayor of Belley for wanting to eliminate "documentary news scenes," going on to say that it was "the filmed news item [le fait divers filmé] which appeared abominable to him," ostensibly because of its potential emotional effect on susceptible viewers. Instead, he argued, it was precisely their documentary neutrality that made the Bonnot films fundamentally moral. "Only cinema documents [documents cinématographiques], taken with care, with method, will remain like impartial witnesses to these tragic moments."[63] He launched the same critique at Herriot: "if you respect the freedom of the press, respect equally our works of current affairs and information, taken in the same manner as in the newspapers."[64] Indeed, it was precisely the fact that mayors could not tell the difference between news footage, which was seemingly neutral, and dramatic representations of crime that led, in Dureau's view, to the wave of interdictions. "They encompass the same repression for both under the pretext . . . that the representation of 'criminal acts' is contrary to the public order."[65]

The industry's change in tactic was, in part, due to the rationale that mayors gave for their interdictions. Chanot, the mayor of Marseilles, argued that it was precisely because the cinema was a popular spectacle that interdiction was warranted. He claimed,

> there is a difference between cinema and theater. Only adults and people of a certain age go to the theater; the cinema, on the contrary, has

61. Bérenger, 83.
62. Leglise, 30 and Dureau, "De la valeur des arrêtés municipaux contre certains films," *CJ* 5/208 (17 August 1912) : 3
63. Dureau, "Le cinéma tel que le juge la grande presse française," 4.
64. Dureau, "Lettre ouverte à M. Herriot," 4.
65. Dureau, "La liberté de la cinématographie en péril," *CJ* 5/202 (6 July 1912) : 3.

above all a clientele of children. And more so, at the theater, pathos
has nothing in common with the realistic and criminal exhibitions,
with the exploits of our modern Cartouches.[66]

Dureau and other defenders refrained from invoking cinema as a
"theater of the people" since the mayors had used that very argument
to legitimate their interventions. Now, cinema's legitimacy rested on
completely opposite terms—as a form of documentation that, when
properly done, evoked a dispassionate, emotionally neutral audience
response. It was absurd to single out cinema, argued Edmond Benoît-
Lévy, director of the large Omnia-Pathé theatre in Paris, when "everyone can read in the newspapers detailed accounts of these crimes, and
everyone can see drawings and photographs that recall (*se rapporter*)
them."[67]

The 1912 crisis itself, therefore, underscored the ambiguity of cinema's status even among its ardent defenders. In shifting the debate
away from "theater" towards "news," the cinema press ended up in-
advertently supporting the mayor's contention that cinema was not a
legitimate theater but a form of spectacle. In attempting to defuse the
moral culpability of crime films, by claiming that they were a form of
news, Dureau and others in the cinema press ultimately underscored
the mayor's rationale—movies *were* different from theater, and consequently could not be legally classified with them. As the cinema
press glumly recognized, the mayors were using cinema's ambiguous
status as a means of asserting total municipal control. The mayors
of Montpelier and Aix-en-Provence even issued decrees requiring all
films to undergo municipal review before exhibition.[68] "The mayors'
decrees," Dureau concluded, "have blocked and are blocking many
exhibitors from showing certain films: in reality they are organizing
censorship in advance (*une censure préalable*) by requiring exhibitors—as in certain towns—to submit their programs to the approval

66. "Le jugement de Marseille," *CJ* 6/236 (1 March 1913) : 17.

67. Edmond Benoît-Lévy, "En plein arbitraire," *L'écho du cinéma* (5 July 1912) : 1.
Benoît-Lévy (1858–1929) founded France's first professional trade journal for cinema,
Phono-Ciné-Gazette in 1905 and opened the Théâtre de la Cinématographie Pathé in
1906. A lawyer by training, he founded and administered many film organizations and
companies and campaigned for authors' and publishers' rights for film adaptations. See
Jean-Jacques Meusy's entry in the *Encyclopedia of Early Cinema*, ed. Richard Abel
(London: Routledge, 2010), 65–66.

68. Leglise, 30.

of the police commissioner or the municipal administration. That is the peril."[69]

Justifying their actions in the name of public safety, therefore, the mayors sought to assume total municipal control over cinema exhibition and in a few cases, notably in Marseille and Hyères, actually brought suits against particular theater owners. Organizations like the Syndicat des Exploitants cinématographistes du Sud-Est (the Southeastern Cinema Exhibitors' Syndicate) and the Fédération du Midi, the region where most of the decrees occurred, visited the Lyonnais mayor in a fruitless attempt to change his mind, and they subsequently sought legal recourse against Herriot with the Conseil d'État. By the fall of 1912, both the issue of cinema's legal status and its legal jurisdiction were before the courts. In the first case, the mayor of Hyères had brought five charges against one Giraudon, for showing five films "exhibiting criminal acts." In October 1912, a police-court magistrate (juge de paix) recognized the legality of the mayor's action, upholding the cinema's status as a *spectacle de curiosité*. In language similar to Cazeneuve, the judge argued that "cinematic spectacles are only images, the photography of a dramatic work; they are not made for the same audiences . . . they set out rather to excite and sometimes to surprise public curiosity, rather than to elevate and develop the esthetic sentiment of spectators."[70] Although Giraudon won on appeal in February 1913, following the "expert" testimony from a philosophy professor from Toulon that crime films do not provoke criminal behavior, the judge upheld the mayor's power of interdiction, arguing that Giraudon's five films did not, in fact, fall under it.[71] In Marseille, another theater owner was similarly acquitted although, as in Hyères, the judge upheld the mayor's power of interdiction. "The judgment," Dureau argued, "agreed with the Marseille mayor . . . on the validity of his power since it placed cinema in the category of *spectacles de curiosité* and not in that of the legitimate theater."[72]

69. Dureau, "De la valeur des arrêtés municipaux contre certains films," 4.

70. Quoted in Leglise, 31.

71. Dureau, "Deuxième procès! Deuxième victoire! La Féderation du Midi triomphe encore à Hyères," *CJ* 6/236 (1 March 1913) : 3; and "Le jugement d'Hyères," *Le cinéma et l'Écho du cinéma réunis* (28 February 1913) : 4.

72. Dureau, "Un premier pas vers la justice: Le jugement de Marseille," *CJ* 6/233 (3 February 1913) : 4.

While the cinema press celebrated these acquittals as victories against municipal overreach, the rulings gave mayors, and by extension the Republican state, the first legal recognition of their authority over cinema exhibition. In April 1913, the Minister of the Interior issued another circular to the prefects, ordering them to forbid the showing of cinematic representations of recent crimes in their *départements*.[73] Finally, in April 1914, the Conseil d'État ruled in the suit brought against Herriot, definitively placed cinema within the category of *spectacle de curiosité* and therefore upheld the mayors' authority to oversee spectacles based on the 1884 Municipal Law. "Thus by the outbreak of war," Hemming notes, "a firm control had been established by local authorities, and through them by the Minister of Interior, over the exhibition of films."[74]

EPILOGUE

Film censorship in prewar France thus emerged out of a particular cluster of forces and anxieties: a widespread fear of juvenile crime, a redoubtable and vigilant network of moral leagues, an uncertainty as to cinema's nature as theater or spectacle, and, above all, a Republican state that sought to extend its power through regulatory legislation. To miss this context is to fail to appreciate why film censorship took the coordinated form it did—as firm governmental control by the mayors, prefects, and the Minister of the Interior rather than, say, the increasing self-regulation adopted by the US industry in response to a disparate patchwork of state and city censorship and a growing threat of national government intervention.[75] Films, like other forms of spectacle, attracted the attention and ire of moral leagues and public officials who saw them as agents of immorality—encouraging emulative tendencies in young, impressionable minds. In their efforts to defend the medium, however, the cinema press only underscored its ambiguity—was it a "theater of the people" whose main function was to move people, provoking their emotions, or was it a form of "news" that recorded events in a dispassionate, neutral manner? For their opponents, like senators Bérenger and Cazeneuve, the very nature of the

73. Hemmings, 334.
74. Hemmings, 337.
75. Lee Grieveseon, *Policing the Cinema: Movies and Censorship in Early Twentieth-Century America* (Berkeley: University of California Press, 2004). In 1915, an influential U.S. Supreme Court decision upheld the validity of state censorship.

medium—the sensory experience of watching animated images—was inherently corruptible in itself. The nature of cinema, and the effect it had, was thus fraught with as many anxieties as the corrupt, criminal, urban society that its films purported to represent.

It should not be surprising then that the debate over cinema censorship and its inherent immorality would persist even after legal judgments relegated it to *spectacle de curiosité* status. Dureau would still occasionally publish editorials defending cinema against charges of moral corruption, while, on the other side, many were still asserting that very point.[76] In May 1913, *Ciné-journal* reported on the formation of a new Belgian association, the League of Moral Cinema and a column from October mentioned with horror that the mayor of Oran in Algeria had forbid the showing of *Fantômas*.[77] Even the ever-vigilant Bérenger was threatening, in the summer of 1914, to "re-establish censorship on all (including theater) forms of spectacle."[78] And the Republican state itself would continue to extend its control over cinema exhibition. In June 1916, the Minister of the Interior established the first visa system, requiring that all films seeking to be shown in France be approved and issued a visa by a newly-created regulatory commission. In 1919, film censorship passed from the Minister of the Interior to that of Public Information and Fine Arts, which now supervised the regulatory commission. Nonetheless, until well into the 1920s, it was still the crime film and "representations of criminal acts" that caused the greatest controversies and led to most of the municipal decrees.[79] Although never conclusively proven, despite the convictions of moral leagues and mayors, that motion pictures were "the mysterious cause of juvenile criminality" in France, the cinema certainly retained its power to provoke and unnerve.[80]

76. See Dureau, "Le cinéma et la criminalité juvénile," *CJ* 5/233 (18 March 1913) and "La question de la moralité des films et le Congrès de Gand," *CJ* 6/261 (23 August 1913).

77. Dureau, "La Ligue du Cinéma Moral," *CJ* 6/248 (24 May 1913) and "Voilà les bêtises qui recommencent!" *CJ* 6/269 (18 October 1913) : 5.

78. Dureau, "M. Bérenger nous menace du rétablissement de la Censure," *CJ* 7/305 (27 June 1914) : 4.

79. Hemmings, 337–44.

80. Dureau, "Le cinéma et la criminalité juvénile," 3.

Figure 1. Ciné-journal [CJ] 195 - 18 May 1912. Advertisement for "Hors la loi," the youth crime film that contributed to the eruption of municipal cinema closings in the summer of 1912.

Figure 2. CJ 196 - 25 May 1912. Another advertisement for "Hors la loi" in
Ciné-journal.

5ᵉ Année. — N° 201   29 Juin 1912.

Ciné=Journal

Organe Hebdomadaire de l'Industrie Cinématographique
Directeur : G. DUREAU

| ABONNEMENTS : FRANCE
Un an . . . . . . 10 fr.
ÉTRANGER
Un an . . . . . . 12 fr. | Le Numéro : 25 cent.

Paraît le Samedi | Rédaction & Administration
30, Rue Bergère
PARIS
TÉLÉPHONE 484-54 |

Lettre ouverte à M. Herriot, maire de Lyon
et à ses imitateurs

MONSIEUR LE MAIRE,

Vous êtes et chacun salue en vous un lettré délicat, un artiste et un esprit qu'on peut croire libéral. Permettez donc à un directeur de cinéma-théâtre de faire justement appel à vos qualités pour vous présenter quelques doléances au nom de l'art, des lettres et de la liberté!

Vous avez interdit dans les salles de spectacle de Lyon les vues ou exhibitions de toute nature représentant des agissements criminels.

Qu'entendez-vous par ces paroles? Je ne demande qu'à le savoir et vous ne me l'avez jamais dit jusqu'alors. Persuadé qu'il n'y avait pas de censure en France et que Lyon était une ville française, j'ai passé depuis de longues années des millions de mètres de films qui, dramatiques, comiques ou documentaires, représentaient des crimes, des délits ou des gestes manifestement criminels. Tout l'art du théâtre vit des passions humaines et retient, entre toutes, celles qui vont jusqu'au meurtre et se classent hors la loi. Relisez un peu vos classiques. Ils ne racontent en vers tragiques que les épouvantables forfaits des légendaires grecs travestis en personnages modernes. Leurs œuvres respirent l'inceste, le meurtre, la trahison et les diverses vilenies qui sont le triste apanage de l'humanité. Quant à nos dramaturges contemporains, ils cultivent âprement sur le même terrain, les mêmes plantes amères pleines de sang et de turpitudes. Nos théâtres, vos théâtres, ne sont point des lieux d'optimisme ni même de simple pudeur : ils sont animés d'une verve réaliste et c'est dire qu'ils n'ouvrent sur le ciel bleu qu'un petit jour de souffrance.

Les scènes comiques elles-mêmes sont pleines « d'agissements criminels » et Gribouille aussi bien que ses collègues du rire fustigent bien souvent l'autorité au nom de laquelle vous prenez aujourd'hui des mesures, — sans doute démesurées. Il n'est pas jusqu'à votre délicieux Guignol Lyonnais qui, rossant le commissaire ou l'huissier, ne donne aux enfants le spectacle le plus démoralisant qui soit au monde.

Figure 3. CJ 201 - 29 June 1912. Lead editorial by Georges Dureau to the Mayor of Lyon, "an open letter to Edouard Herriot."

5ᵉ Année. — Nº 202   6 Juillet 1912

Ciné=Journal

Organe Hebdomadaire de l'Industrie Cinématographique
Directeur : G. DUREAU

ABONNEMENTS ; FRANCE	Le Numéro : 25 cent.	Rédaction & Administration
Un an . . . . . . 10 fr.	☁	30, Rue Bergère
ÉTRANGER		PARIS
Un an . . . . . . 12 fr.	¿Paraît le Samedi	TÉLÉPHONE

La Liberté de la Cinématographie en péril

ALERTE !

En vérité, la contagion des idées fausses est plus grave encore que celle des idées justes. Il y a quelques semaines, le maire de Belley (Ain), ayant cru devoir interdire un film d'actualité qui retraçait, après tous les journaux de France, la capture de Bonnot, le journal le *Temps* s'empressa de signaler son geste comme un « exemple » à tous les maires de France. Le conseil du grand quotidien ne tarda pas à être écouté. Plusieurs magistrats municipaux — et non des moindres — MM. Herriot, de Lyon; Chanot, de Marseille; X..., de Remiremont; Z..., de Bordeaux, et Y..., d'Ixelles, en Brabant, se ruèrent avec frénésie dans le sentier de la morale que leur indiquait avec persuasion le doigt quelque peu autoritaire de M. Hébrard. Une grande confusion s'en suivit. Ces honorables représentants des libertés municipales ne surent pas distinguer entre nos films de reportage et les œuvres de composition dramatique. Ils englobèrent dans la même répression les uns et les autres, sous le prétexte — un peu tardif — que la représentation des

« agissements criminels » était contraire à l'ordre public et qu'il était de leur pouvoir de la proscrire.

La question n'est pas de celles qu'on peut résoudre d'un trait de plume, et la simple raison, sœur du bon sens, n'y suffirait même pas. Je laisse donc aux autorités du Conseil d'État et de la Cour de Cassation le soin de prononcer légalement, au nom du droit, sur la valeur de cette censure municipale. Nous saurons bientôt s'il y a dans cette affaire et dans ces mesures préventives quelque excès de pouvoir.

Mais en attendant, à l'heure où tous les cinématographistes conscients, soucieux de l'avenir et désireux de leur liberté commerciale, affirment par leurs lettres et leurs propos personnels la nécessité de grouper leurs forces sur la défensive, nous avons le regret de voir passer à l'ennemi — du côté de la grande presse hostile à nos progrès — un de nos confrères professionnels. Et notre regret s'augmente lorsque nous constatons que le jeune Syndicat des Directeurs de Cinémas français — pour une misérable

Figure 4. CJ 202 - 6 July 1912. Another Dureau editorial, underscoring the panic that the wave of municipal theater closings was causing in the cinema industry.

Contributors

RICHARD ABEL is the Robert Altman Collegiate Professor of Film Studies in the Department of Screen Art & Cultures at the University of Michigan and served as Chair of the Department (2005–09). He has published essays in dozens of journals and has edited and published numerous books on film studies. His books include *French Cinema: The First Wave, 1915–1929* (Princeton, 1984), *French Film Theory and Criticism, 1907–1939: A History/ Anthology in Two Volumes* (Princeton, 1988); *The Ciné Goes to Town: French Cinema, 1896–1914* (California, 1994); *Silent Film* (Rutgers, 1996); *The Red Rooster Scare: Making Cinema American 1900–1910* (California, 1999) and *Americanizing the Movies and "Movie Mad" Audiences, 1900–1910* (California, 2006). He also served as general editor of the *Encyclopedia of Early Cinema* (Routledge, 2005), a paperback edition of which appeared in 2010.

KAREN L. CARTER is assistant professor of art history at the Kendall School of Art and Design at Ferris State University. She has published "L'âge de l'affiche: Critics, Collectors and Urban Contexts," the principal essay for the exhibition catalogue *Toulouse-Lautrec and the French Imprint: Sources and Legacies of Fin-de-Siècle Posters, Paris—Brussels—Barcelona*, as well as essays in *Early Popular Visual Culture* (2010) and the *Journal of Design History* (2012). She is currently writing a book about the critical reception, display, and spectatorship of illustrated posters. . She has received awards and fellowships from the National Endowment for the Arts, the Getty Research Institute, the French-American Foundation in New York, and the Library of Congress.

DONALD E. ENGLISH is a historian of French culture and politics who received his Ph.D. in Modern European History from the Uni-

YFS 122, *Out of Sight: Political Censorship of the Visual Arts in Nineteenth-Century France*, ed. Goldstein, © 2012 by Yale University.

versity of Washington. He has taught and served as an administrator for colleges and universities in Colorado, Virginia, Washington, California, and abroad; he recently retired as Dean of the
Division of Continuing Education at Colorado State University,
Pueblo. A specialist in visual culture and the history of photography, his publications include *The Political uses of Photography
in the Third French Republic, 1981–1914* (UMI Research Press,
1984) and numerous articles on the history of French photography.
He is the recipient of fellowships and awards from the American
Council of Learned Societies and the National Endowment for the
Humanities.

KENNETH GARNER is a Ph.D. candidate in the Department of History
and a graduate certificate student in the Department of Screen
Arts and Cultures at the University of Michigan. His research interests focus on the relationship of French cinema to the state,
specifically in the area of education.

ROBERT JUSTIN GOLDSTEIN is the author of numerous books and articles on nineteenth-century European censorship, including *Political Censorship of the Arts and the Press in Nineteenth-Century
Europe* (1989). He is professor emeritus of political science at Oak-
land University and currently a research associate at the University of Michigan at Ann Arbor.

DONALD NICHOLSON-SMITH has translated many works from the
French, among them Apollinaire's *Letters to Madeleine*, Artaud's
50 Drawings to Murder Magic, Guy Debord's *The Society of the
Spectacle*, Jean-Patrick Manchette's *Fatale*, and, with Alyson Wa-
ters, Yasmina Khadra's *Cousin K*. His new translation of Raoul
Vaneigem's *The Revolution of Everyday Life* is forthcoming with
PM Press. A native of Manchester, England, he now lives in Brook-
lyn, New York.

DAVID O'BRIEN teaches at the University of Illinois at Urbana-
Champaign. He is the author of *After the Revolution: Antoine-
Jean Gros, Painting and Propaganda under Napoleon* (2006, also
translated into French , 2006). His article, "Another lieu de mem-
oire? Napoleonic Painting, the Museum and Memory," recently
appeared in *War Memories: The Revolutionary and Napoleonic
Wars in Modern European Culture* (2012). He is currently fin-
ishing a book on the theme of civilization in the art of Eugène
Delacroix.

BERTRAND TILLIER, Docteur, Université de Paris I (Panthéon-Sorbonne), holds the positions of Professor of Contemporary Art History at the Université de Bourgogne and Researcher at the Centre Georges Chevrier (Unité Mixte de Recherche 5605). His work is concerned mainly with the relationship between art and politics and with the history of caricature in the nineteenth and twentieth centuries. His publications include *La RépubliCature, la caricature politique en France (1870–1914)*(Paris: CNRS, 1997 [new edition, 2002]); *La Commune de Paris, révolution sans images! Politique et représentations dans la France républicaine (1871–1914)* (Seyssel: Champ Vallon, 2004); *Les artistes et l'affaire Dreyfus (1898–1908)* (Seyssel: Champ Vallon, 2009); and, with Aude Fauvel, *André Gill, Derniers dessins d'un fou à lier* (Tusson: Éditions Du Lérot, 2010).

JUDITH WECHSLER is an art historian of nineteenth-century French art and makes films on art. Her books include *Daumier. Le Cabinet des dessins; A Human Comedy: Physiognomy and Caricature in 19th-Century Paris* and *The Interpretation of Cézanne*. She has written numerous articles on Daumier, most recently working on Daumier's use of Allegory, and Daumier's Saltimbanques. Wechsler has made 25 films on art, most notably *Rachel of the Comédie-Francaise* (with the Comédie Francaise), *Drawing, the Thinking Hand* (for the Louvre), *Jasper Johns: Take an Object* (with Hans Namuth), *Daumier: One Must Be of One's Time* and *Daumier, Paris and the Spectator* (with Charles Eames) and has won various awards at film festivals. Currently, she is working on a film on Walter Benjamin. She is the National Endowment for the Humanities Professor at Tufts, emerita, taught at MIT and RISD, and has been visiting professor at Harvard, the École normale supérieure in Paris, the University of Paris, and the Hebrew University. Wechsler has received 6 National Endowment for the Humanities Grants, and 2 National Endowment for the Arts awards and was decorated by the French government as Chevalier de l'ordre des arts et des letters.

Yale French Studies is the oldest English-language journal in the United States devoted to French and Francophone literature and culture. Each volume is conceived and organized by a guest editor or editors around a particular theme or author. Interdisciplinary approaches are particularly welcome, as are contributions from scholars and writers from around the world. Recent volumes have been devoted to a wide variety of subjects, among them: Levinas; Perec; Paulhan; Haiti; Belgium; Crime Fiction; Surrealism; Material Culture in Medieval and Renaissance France; and French Education.

Yale French Studies is published twice yearly by Yale University Press (yalebooks.com) and may be accessed on JSTOR (jstor.org).

For information on how to submit a proposal for a volume of *Yale French Studies,* visit yale.edu/french and click "Yale French Studies."